P9-CEY-261

Also by Elie Wiesel

Dawn

Day

In memory of
my parents and of my little sister,
Tzipora

Night

Elie Wiesel

with Connections

HOLT, RINEHART AND WINSTON
Harcourt Brace & Company
Austin • New York • Orlando • Atlanta • San Francisco
Boston • Dallas • Toronto • London

For permission to reprint copyrighted material, grateful acknowledgment is made to the following sources:

Hill and Wang, a division of Farrar, Straus & Giroux, Inc.: *Night* by Elie Wiesel, translated by Stella Rodway. Translation copyright © 1960 by MacGibbon and Kee; copyright renewed © 1988 by The Collins Publishing Group. All rights reserved.

Beacon Press: Excerpt (retitled "An Inner Freedom") from "Experiences in a Concentration Camp" from *Man's Search for Meaning: An Introduction to Logotherapy,* Third Edition, by Viktor E. Frankl. Copyright © 1959, 1962, 1984 by Viktor Frankl. ***The Boston Globe:*** Excerpt (retitled "Why *Do* They Visit? A Look at the Success of the United States Holocaust Memorial Museum") from "Why Do They Come? American Innocence Confronts the Holocaust Museum" by John Aloysius Farrell from *The Boston Globe,* September 11, 1994. Copyright © 1994 by The Boston Globe. ***Doubleday, a division of Random House, Inc.:*** "Babii Yar," translated by George Reavey from *Twentieth Century Russian Poetry: Silver and Steel, an Anthology,* selected and with an introduction by Yevgeny Yevtushenko; edited by Albert C. Todd and Max Hayward, with Daniel Weissbort. Copyright © 1993 by Doubleday, a division of Random House, Inc. ***Facing History and Ourselves:*** From "Mauthausen May 1945" from *I Promised I Would Tell* by Sonia Schreiber Weitz, edited by Susan Belt Cogley. Copyright © 1993 by Sonia Schreiber Weitz. ***Farrar, Straus & Giroux, LLC:*** "But in the Night" from *The Seeker* by Nelly Sachs, translated by Ruth and Matthew Mead. Translation copyright © 1970 and renewed © 1998 by Farrar, Straus & Giroux, Inc. ***The Jewish Publication Society:*** "The Treblinka Revolt" by Stanislaw Kohn, and "The Yellow Star" by S. B. Unsdorfer, translated from the Yiddish by Joseph Leftwich, from *Anthology of Holocaust Literature,* edited by Jacob Glatstein, Israel Knox, and Samuel Margoshes. Copyright © 1968 by The Jewish Publication Society of America. ***Newsweek, Inc.:*** From "War Crimes: Lessons of Nuremberg" (retitled "The Trial of the Century") from *Newsweek,* November 6, 1995. Copyright © 1995 by Newsweek, Inc. ***Nobel Foundation:*** Nobel Peace Prize Acceptance Speech by Elie Wiesel, December 10, 1986. Copyright © 1986 by The Nobel Foundation. ***Oxford University Press, Inc.:*** "The Berlin-Bucharest Express" from *Hasidic Tales of the Holocaust* by Yaffa Eliach. Copyright © 1982 by Yaffa Eliach. ***Pantheon Books, a division of Random House, Inc.:*** From Chapter Two, "Auschwitz (Time Flies)" *The Complete Maus: A Survivor's Tale* by Art Spiegelman. Copyright © 1973, 1980, 1981, 1982, 1983, 1984, 1985, and 1986 by Art Spiegelman. ***The Rabbinical Council of America, Inc.:*** "Mourner's Kaddish" from *The Traditional Prayer Book for Sabbath and Festivals,* edited and translated by David De Sola Pool. Copyright © 1960 by The Rabbinical Council of America, Inc. ***The Seattle Times Co.:*** Excerpt (retitled "A Cambodian Nightmare") from "Cambodian Refugees: Time and Distance Can't Bury Memories of the Killing Fields" by Alex Tizon from *The Seattle Times/Post-Intelligencer,* January 23, 1994. Copyright © 1994 by The Seattle Times. ***Writer's House, Inc.:*** "A Spring Morning" by Ida Fink from *A Scrap of Time,* translated by Madeline G. Levine. Copyright © 1987 by Ida Fink.

Cover Art: Joe Melomo

Printed in the United States of America

ISBN 0-03-055462-4

23 24 25 043 09 08

Contents

CONTINUED

They called him Moché the Beadle, as though he had never had a surname in his life. He was a man of all work at a Hasidic synagogue. The Jews of Sighet—that little town in Transylvania where I spent my childhood—were very fond of him. He was very poor and lived humbly. Generally my fellow townspeople, though they would help the poor, were not particularly fond of them. Moché the Beadle was the exception. Nobody ever felt embarrassed by him. Nobody ever felt encumbered by his presence. He was a past master in the art of making himself insignificant, of seeming invisible.

Physically he was as awkward as a clown. He made people smile, with his waiflike timidity. I loved his great, dreaming eyes, their gaze lost in the distance. He spoke little. He used to sing, or, rather, to chant. Such snatches as you could hear told of the suffering of the divinity, of the Exile of Providence, who, according to the cabbala, awaits his deliverance in that of man.

I got to know him toward the end of 1941. I was twelve. I believed profoundly. During the day I studied the Talmud, and at night I ran to the synagogue to weep over the destruction of the Temple.

One day I asked my father to find me a master to guide me in my studies of the cabbala.

"You're too young for that. Maimonides said it was only at thirty that one had the right to venture into the perilous world of mysticism. You must first study the basic subjects within your own understanding."

My father was a cultured, rather unsentimental man. There was never any display of emotion, even at home. He was more concerned with others than with his own family. The Jewish community in Sighet held him in the greatest esteem. They often used to consult him about public matters and even about private ones. There were four of us children: Hilda, the eldest; then Béa; I was the third, and the only son; the baby of the family was Tzipora.

My parents ran a shop. Hilda and Béa helped them with the work. As for me, they said my place was at school.

"There aren't any cabbalists at Sighet," my father would repeat.

He wanted to drive the notion out of my head. But it was in vain. I found a master for myself, Moché the Beadle.

He had noticed me one day at dusk, when I was praying.

"Why do you weep when you pray?" he asked me, as though he had known me a long time.

"I don't know why," I answered, greatly disturbed.

The question had never entered my head. I wept because—because of something inside me that felt the need for tears. That was all I knew.

"Why do you pray?" he asked me, after a moment.

Why did I pray? A strange question. Why did I live? Why did I breathe?

"I don't know why," I said, even more distrubed and ill at ease. "I don't know why."

After that day I saw him often. He explained to me

with great insistence that every question possessed a power that did not lie in the answer.

"Man raises himself toward God by the questions he asks Him," he was fond of repeating. "That is the true dialogue. Man questions God and God answers. But we don't understand His answers. We can't understand them. Because they come from the depths of the soul, and they stay there until death. You will find the true answers, Eliezer, only within yourself!"

"And why do you pray, Moché?" I asked him.

"I pray to the God within me that He will give me the strength to ask Him the right questions."

We talked like this nearly every evening. We used to stay in the synagogue after all the faithful had left, sitting in the gloom, where a few half-burned candles still gave a flickering light.

One evening I told him how unhappy I was because I could not find a master in Sighet to instruct me in the Zohar, the cabbalistic books, the secrets of Jewish mysticism. He smiled indulgently. After a long silence, he said:

"There are a thousand and one gates leading into the orchard of mystical truth. Every human being has his own gate. We must never make the mistake of wanting to enter the orchard by any gate but our own. To do this is dangerous for the one who enters and also for those who are already there."

And Moché the Beadle, the poor barefoot of Sighet, talked to me for long hours of the revelations and mysteries of the cabbala. It was with him that my initiation began. We would read together, ten times over, the same page of the Zohar. Not to learn it by heart, but to extract the divine essence from it.

And throughout those evenings a conviction grew in me that Moché the Beadle would draw me with him into eternity, into that time where question and answer would become *one*.

Then one day they expelled all the foreign Jews from Sighet. And Moché the Beadle was a foreigner.

Crammed into cattle trains by Hungarian police, they wept bitterly. We stood on the platform and wept too. The train disappeared on the horizon; it left nothing behind but its thick, dirty smoke.

I heard a Jew behind me heave a sigh.

"What can we expect?" he said. "It's war. . . ."

The deportees were soon forgotten. A few days after they had gone, people were saying that they had arrived in Galicia, were working there, and were even satisfied with their lot.

Several days passed. Several weeks. Several months. Life had returned to normal. A wind of calmness and reassurance blew through our houses. The traders were doing good business, the students lived buried in their books, and the children played in the streets.

One day, as I was just going into the synagogue, I saw, sitting on a bench near the door, Moché the Beadle.

He told his story and that of his companions. The train full of deportees had crossed the Hungarian frontier and on Polish territory had been taken in charge by the Gestapo. There it had stopped. The Jews had to get out and climb into lorries. The lorries drove toward a forest. The Jews were made to get out. They were made to dig huge graves. And when they had finished their work, the Gestapo began theirs. Without passion, without haste, they slaughtered their prisoners. Each one had to go up to the hole and present his neck. Babies were thrown into the air and the machine gunners used them as targets. This was in the forest of Galicia, near Kolomaye. How had Moché the Beadle escaped? Miraculously. He was wounded in the leg and taken for dead. . . .

Through long days and nights, he went from one Jewish house to another, telling the story of Malka, the young girl who had taken three days to die, and of Tobias, the tailor, who had begged to be killed before his sons. . . .

Moché had changed. There was no longer any joy in his eyes. He no longer sang. He no longer talked to me of God or the cabbala, but only of what he had seen. People refused not only to believe his stories, but even to listen to them.

"He's just trying to make us pity him. What an imagination he has!" they said. Or even: "Poor fellow. He's gone mad."

And as for Moché, he wept.

"Jews, listen to me. It's all I ask of you. I don't want money or pity. Only listen to me," he would cry between prayers at dusk and the evening prayers.

I did not believe him myself. I would often sit with him in the evening after the service, listening to his stories and trying my hardest to understand his grief. I felt only pity for him.

"They take me for a madman," he would whisper, and tears, like drops of wax, flowed from his eyes.

Once, I asked him this question:

"Why are you so anxious that people should believe what you say. In your place, I shouldn't care whether they believed me or not. . . ."

He closed his eyes, as though to escape time.

"You don't understand," he said in despair. "You can't understand. I have been saved miraculously. I managed to get back here. Where did I get the strength from? I wanted to come back to Sighet to tell you the story of my death. So that you could prepare yourselves while there was still time. To live? I don't attach my importance to my life any more. I'm alone. No, I wanted to come back, and to warn you. And see how it is, no one will listen to me. . . ."

That was toward the end of 1942. Afterward life returned to normal. The London radio, which we listened to every evening, gave us heartening news: the daily bombardment of Germany; Stalingrad; preparation for the second front. And we, the Jews of Sighet, were waiting for better days, which would not be long in coming now.

I continued to devote myself to my studies. By day, the Talmud, at night, the cabbala. My father was occupied with his business and the doings of the community. My grandfather had come to celebrate the New Year with us, so that he could attend the services of the famous rabbi of Borsche. My mother began to think that it was high time to find a suitable young man for Hilda.

Thus the year 1943 passed by.

Spring 1944. Good news from the Russian front. No doubt could remain now of Germany's defeat. It was only a question of time—of months or weeks perhaps.

The trees were in blossom. This was a year like any other, with its springtime, its betrothals, its weddings and births.

People said: "The Russian army's making gigantic strides forward . . . Hitler won't be able to do us any harm, even if he wants to."

Yes, we even doubted that he wanted to exterminate us.

Was he going to wipe out a whole people? Could he exterminate a population scattered throughout so many countries? So many millions! What methods could he use? And in the middle of the twentieth century!

Besides, people were interested in everything—in strategy, in diplomacy, in politics, in Zionism—but not in their own fate.

Even Moché the Beadle was silent. He was weary of speaking. He wandered in the synagogue or in the streets, with his eyes down, his back bent, avoiding people's eyes.

At that time, it was still possible to obtain emigration permits for Palestine. I had asked my father to sell out, liquidate his business, and leave.

"I'm too old, my son," he replied. "I'm too old to start a new life. I'm too old to start from scratch again in a country so far away. . . ."

The Budapest radio announced that the Fascist party had come into power. Horthy had been forced to ask one of the leaders of the Nyilas party to form a new government.

Still this was not enough to worry us. Of course we had heard about the Fascists, but they were still just an abstraction to us. This was only a change in the administration.

The following day, there was more disturbing news: with government permission, German troops had entered Hungarian territory.

Here and there, anxiety was aroused. One of our friends, Berkovitz, who had just returned from the capital, told us:

"The Jews in Budapest are living in an atmosphere of fear and terror. There are anti-Semitic incidents every day, in the streets, in the trains. The Fascists are attacking Jewish shops and synagogues. The situation is getting very serious."

This news spread like wildfire through Sighet. Soon it was on everyone's lips. But not for long. Optimism soon revived.

"The Germans won't get as far as this. They'll stay in Budapest. There are strategic and political reasons. . . ."

Before three days had passed, German army cars had appeared in our streets.

Anguish. German soldiers—with their steel helmets, and their emblem, the death's head.

However, our first impressions of the Germans were most reassuring. The officers were billeted in private houses, even in the homes of Jews. Their attitude toward their hosts was distant, but polite. They never demanded the impossible, made no unpleasant comments, and even smiled occasionally at the mistress of the house. One German officer lived in the house opposite ours. He had a room with the Kahn family. They said he was a charming man—calm, likable, polite, and sympathetic. Three days after he moved in he brought Madame Kahn a box of chocolates. The optimists rejoiced.

"Well, there you are, you see! What did we tell you? You wouldn't believe us. There they are *your* Germans! What do you think of them? Where is their famous cruelty?"

The Germans were already in the town, the Fascists were already in power, the verdict had already been pronounced, yet the Jews of Sighet continued to smile.

The week of Passover. The weather was wonderful. My mother bustled round her kitchen. There were no longer any synagogues open. We gathered in private houses: the Germans were not to be provoked. Practically every rabbi's flat became a house of prayer.

We drank, we ate, we sang. The Bible bade us rejoice during the seven days of the feast, to be happy. But our hearts were not in it. Our hearts had been beating more rapidly for some days. We wished the feast were over, so that we should not have to play this comedy any longer.

On the seventh day of Passover the curtain rose. The Germans arrested the leaders of the Jewish community.

From that moment, everything happened very quickly. The race toward death had begun.

The first step: Jews would not be allowed to leave their houses for three days—on pain of death.

Moché the Beadle came running to our house.

"I warned you," he cried to my father. And, without waiting for a reply, he fled.

That same day the Hungarian police burst into all the Jewish houses in the street. A Jew no longer had the right to keep in his house gold, jewels, or any objects of value. Everything had to be handed over to the authorities—on pain of death. My father went down into the cellar and buried our savings.

At home, my mother continued to busy herself with her usual tasks. At times she would pause and gaze at us, silent.

When the three days were up, there was a new decree: every Jew must wear the yellow star.

Some of the prominent members of the community came to see my father—who had highly placed connections in the Hungarian police—to ask him what he thought of the situation. My father did not consider it so grim—but perhaps he did not want to dishearten the others or rub salt in their wounds:

"The yellow star? Oh well, what of it? You don't die of it. . . ."

(Poor Father! Of what then did you die?)

But already they were issuing new decrees. We were no longer allowed to go into restaurants or cafés, to travel on the railway, to attend the synagogue, to go out into the street after six o'clock.

Then came the ghetto.

Two ghettos were set up in Sighet. A large one, in the center of the town, occupied four streets, and another smaller one extended over several small side streets in the outlying district. The street where we lived, Serpent Street, was inside the first ghetto. We still lived, therefore, in our own house. But as it was at the corner, the windows facing the outside street had to be blocked up. We gave up some of our rooms to relatives who had been driven out of their flats.

Little by little life returned to normal. The barbed wire which fenced us in did not cause us any real fear. We even thought ourselves rather well off; we were entirely self-contained. A little Jewish republic. . . . We appointed a Jewish Council, a Jewish police, an office for social assistance, a labor committee, a hygiene department—a whole government machinery.

Everyone marveled at it. We should no longer have before our eyes those hostile faces, those hate-laden stares. Our fear and anguish were at an end. We were living among Jews, among brothers. . . .

Of course, there were still some unpleasant moments. Every day the Germans came to fetch men to stoke coal on the military trains. There were not many volunteers for work of this kind. But apart from that the atmosphere was peaceful and reassuring.

The general opinion was that we were going to remain in the ghetto until the end of the war, until the arrival of the Red Army. Then everything would be as before. It was neither German nor Jew who ruled the ghetto—it was illusion.

On the Saturday before Pentecost, in the spring sunshine, people strolled, carefree and unheeding, through the swarming streets. They chatted happily. The children played games on the pavements. With some of my schoolmates, I sat in the Ezra Malik gardens, studying a treatise on the Talmud.

Night fell. There were twenty people gathered in our back yard. My father was telling them anecdotes and expounding his own views on the situation. He was a good story teller.

Suddenly the gate opened and Stern—a former tradesman who had become a policeman—came in and took my father aside. Despite the gathering dusk, I saw my father turn pale.

"What's the matter?" we all asked him.

"I don't know. I've been summoned to an extraordinary meeting of the council. Something must have happened."

The good story he had been in the middle of telling us was to remain unfinished.

"I'm going there," he went on. "I shall be back as soon as I can. I'll tell you all about it. Wait for me."

We were prepared to wait for some hours. The back yard became like the hall outside an operating room. We were only waiting for the door to open—to see the opening of the firmament itself. Other neighbors, having heard rumors, had come to join us. People looked at their watches. The time passed very slowly. What could such a long meeting mean?

"I've got a premonition of evil," said my mother. "This afternoon I noticed some new faces in the ghetto—two German officers, from the Gestapo, I believe. Since we've been here, not a single officer has ever shown himself. . . ."

It was nearly midnight. No one had wanted to go to bed. A few people had paid a flying visit to their homes to see that everything was all right. Others had returned home, but they left instructions that they were to be told as soon as my father came back.

At last the door opened and he appeared. He was pale. At once he was surrounded.

"What happened? Tell us what happened! Say something!"

How avid we were at that moment for one word of confidence, one sentence to say that there were no grounds for fear, that the meeting could not have been more commonplace, more routine, that it had only been a question of social welfare, of sanitary arrangements! But one glance at my father's haggard face was enough.

"I have terrible news," he said at last. "Deportation."

The ghetto was to be completely wiped out. We were to leave street by street, starting the following day.

We wanted to know everything, all the details. The news had stunned everyone, yet we wanted to drain the bitter draft to the dregs.

"Where are we being taken?"

This was a secret. A secret from all except one: the President of the Jewish Council. But he would not say; he *could* not say. The Gestapo had threatened to shoot him if he talked.

"There are rumors going around," said my father in a broken voice, "that we're going somewhere in Hungary, to work in the brick factories. Apparently, the reason is that the front is too close here. . . ."

And, after a moment's silence, he added:

"Each person will be allowed to take only his own personal belongings. A bag on our backs, some food, a few clothes. Nothing else."

Again a heavy silence.

"Go and wake the neighbors up," said my father. "So that they can get ready."

The shadows beside me awoke as from a long sleep. They fled, silently, in all directions.

For a moment we were alone. Then suddenly Batia Reich, a relative who was living with us, came into the room:

"There's someone knocking on the blocked-up window, the one that faces outside!"

It was not until after the war that I learned who it was that had knocked. It was an inspector in the Hungarian police, a friend of my father. Before we went into the ghetto, he had said to us: "Don't worry. If you're in any danger, I'll warn you." If he could have spoken to us that evening, we could perhaps have fled. . . . But by the time we had managed to open the window, it was too late. There was no one outside.

The ghetto awoke. One by one, lights came on in the windows.

I went into the house of one of my father's friends. I woke up the head of the household, an old man with a gray beard and the eyes of a dreamer. He was stooped from long nights of study.

"Get up, sir, get up! You've got to get ready for the journey! You're going to be expelled from here tomorrow with your whole family, and all the rest of the Jews. Where to? Don't ask me, sir. Don't ask me any questions. Only God could answer you. For heaven's sake, get up."

He had not understood a word of what I was saying. He probably thought I had gone out of my mind.

"What tale is this? Get ready for the journey? What journey? Why? What's going on? Have you gone mad?"

Still half asleep, he stared at me with terror-stricken eyes, as though he expected me to burst out laughing and say in the end, "Get back to bed. Go to sleep. Pleasant dreams. Nothing's happened at all. It was just a joke."

My throat was dry, the words choked in it, paralyzing my lips. I could not say any more.

Then he understood. He got out of bed and with automatic movements began to get dressed. Then he went up to the bed where his wife slept and touched her brow with infinite tenderness; she opened her eyes, and it seemed to me that her lips were brushed by a smile. Then he went to his children's beds and woke them swiftly, dragging them from their dreams. I fled.

Time passed very quickly. It was already four o'clock in the morning. My father ran to right and left, exhausted, comforting friends, running to the Jewish Council to see if the edict had not been revoked in the meantime. To the very last moment, a germ of hope stayed alive in our hearts.

The women were cooking eggs, roasting meat, baking cakes, and making knapsacks. The children wandered all over the place, hanging their heads, not knowing what to do with themselves, where to go, to keep from getting in the way of the grown-ups. Our back yard had become a real market place. Household treasures, valuable carpets, silver candelabra, prayer books, Bibles, and other religious articles littered the dusty ground beneath a wonderfully blue sky; pathetic objects which looked as though they had never belonged to anyone.

By eight o'clock in the morning, a weariness like molten lead began to settle in the veins, the limbs, the brain. I was in the midst of my prayers when suddenly there were shouts in the street. I tore myself from my phylacteries and ran to the window. Hungarian police had entered the ghetto and were shouting in the neighboring street:

"All Jews outside! Hurry!"

Some Jewish police went into the houses, saying in broken voices:

"The time's come now . . . you've got to leave all this. . . ."

The Hungarian police struck out with truncheons and rifle butts, to right and left, without reason, indiscriminately, their blows falling upon old men and women, children and invalids alike.

One by one the houses emptied, and the street filled with people and bundles. By ten o'clock, all the condemned were outside. The police took a roll call, once twice, twenty times. The heat was intense. Sweat streamed from faces and bodies.

Children cried for water.

Water? There was plenty, close at hand, in the houses, in the yards, but they were forbidden to break the ranks.

"Water! Mummy! Water!"

The Jewish police from the ghetto were able to go and fill a few jugs secretly. Since my sisters and I were destined for the last convoy and we were still allowed to move about, we helped them as well as we could.

Then, at last, at one o'clock in the afternoon, came the signal to leave.

There was joy—yes, joy. Perhaps they thought that God could have devised no torment in hell worse than that of sitting there among the bundles, in the middle of the road, beneath a blazing sun; that anything would be preferable to that. They began their journey without a backward glance at the abandoned streets, the dead, empty houses, the gardens, the tombstones. . . . On everyone's back was a pack. In everyone's eyes was suffering drowned in tears. Slowly, heavily, the procession made its way to the gate of the ghetto.

And there was I, on the pavement, unable to make a move. Here came the Rabbi, his back bent, his face shaved, his pack on his back. His mere presence among the deportees added a touch of unreality to the scene. It was like a page torn from some story book, from some historical novel about the captivity of Babylon or the Spanish Inquisition.

One by one they passed in front of me, teachers, friends, others, all those I had been afraid of, all those I once could have laughed at, all those I had lived with over the years. They went by, fallen, dragging their packs, dragging their lives, deserting their homes, the years of their childhood, cringing like beaten dogs.

They passed without a glance in my direction. They must have envied me.

The procession disappeared round the corner of the street. A few paces farther on, and they would have passed beyond the ghetto walls.

The street was like a market place that had suddenly been abandoned. Everything could be found there: suitcases, portfolios, briefcases, knives, plates, banknotes, papers, faded portraits. All those things that people had thought of taking with them, and which in the end they had left behind. They had lost all value.

Everywhere rooms lay open. Doors and windows gaped onto the emptiness. Everything was free for anyone, belonging to nobody. It was simply a matter of helping oneself. An open tomb.

A hot summer sun.

We had spent the day fasting. But we were not very hungry. We were exhausted.

My father had accompanied the deportees as far as the entrance of the ghetto. They first had to go through the big synagogue, where they were minutely searched, to see that they were not taking away any gold, silver, or other objects of value. There were outbreaks of hysteria and blows with the truncheons.

"When is our turn coming?" I asked my father.

"The day after tomorrow. At least—at least, unless things turn out differently. A miracle, perhaps . . . ."

Where were the people being taken to? Didn't anyone know yet? No, the secret was well kept.

Night had fallen. That evening we went to bed early. My father said:

"Sleep well, children. It's not until the day after tomorrow, Tuesday."

Monday passed like a small summer cloud, like a dream in the first daylight hours.

Busy with getting our packs ready, with baking bread and cakes, we no longer thought of anything. The verdict had been delivered.

That evening, our mother made us go to bed very early, to conserve our strength, she said. It was our last night at home.

I was up at dawn. I wanted time to pray before we were expelled.

My father had got up earlier to go and seek information. He came back at about eight o'clock. Good news: it wasn't today that we were leaving the town. We were only to move into the little ghetto. There we would wait for the last transport. We should be the last to leave.

At nine o'clock, Sunday's scenes began all over again. Policemen with truncheons yelling:

"All Jews outside!"

We were ready. I was the first to leave. I did not want to see my parents' faces. I did not want to break into tears. We stayed sitting down in the middle of the road, as the others had done the day before yesterday. There was the same infernal heat. The same thirst. But there was no longer anyone left to bring us water.

I looked at our house, where I had spent so many years in my search for God; in fasting in order to hasten the coming of the Messiah; in imagining what my life would be like. Yet I felt little sorrow. I thought of nothing.

"Get up! Count off!"

Standing. Counting off. Sitting down. Standing up again. On the ground once more. Endlessly. We waited impatiently to be fetched. What were they waiting for? At last the order came:

"Forward march!"

My father wept. It was the first time I had ever seen him weep. I had never imagined that he could. As for my mother, she walked with a set expression on her face, without a word, deep in thought. I looked at my little sister Tzipora, her fair hair well combed, a red coat over her arm, a little girl of seven. The bundle on her back was too heavy for her. She gritted her teeth. She knew by now that it would be useless to complain. The police were striking out with their truncheons. "Faster!" I had no strength left. The journey had only just begun, and I felt so weak. . . .

"Faster! Faster! Get on with you, lazy swine!" yelled the Hungarian police.

It was from that moment that I began to hate them, and

my hate is still the only link between us today. They were our first oppressors. They were the first of the faces of hell and death.

We were ordered to run. We advanced in double time. Who would have thought we were so strong? Behind their windows, behind their shutters, our compatriots looked out at us as we passed.

At last we reached our destination. Throwing our bags to the ground, we sank down:

"Oh God, Lord of the Universe, take pity upon us in Thy great mercy. . . ."

The little ghetto. Three days before, people had still been living there—the people who owned the things we were using now. They had been expelled. Already we had completely forgotten them.

The disorder was greater than in the big ghetto. The people must have been driven out unexpectedly. I went to see the rooms where my uncle's family had lived. On the table there was a half-finished bowl of soup. There was a pie waiting to be put in the oven. Books were littered about on the floor. Perhaps my uncle had had dreams of taking them with him?

We settled in. (What a word!) I went to get some wood; my sisters lit the fire. Despite her own weariness, my mother began to prepare a meal.

"We must keep going, we must keep going," she kept on repeating.

The people's morale was not too bad; we were beginning to get used to the situation. In the street, they even went so far as to have optimistic conversations. The Boche would not have time to expel us, they were saying . . . as far as those who had already been deported were concerned, it was too bad; no more could be done. But they would probably allow us to live out our wretched little lives here, until the end of the war.

The ghetto was not guarded. Everyone could come and go as they pleased. Our old servant, Martha, came to see us. Weeping bitterly, she begged us to come to her village, where she could give us a safe refuge. My father did not want to hear of it.

"You can go if you want to," he said to me and to my older sisters. "I shall stay here with your mother and the child. . . ."

Naturally, we refused to be separated.

Night. No one prayed, so that the night would pass quickly. The stars were only sparks of the fire which devoured us. Should that fire die out one day, there would be nothing left in the sky but dead stars, dead eyes.

There was nothing else to do but to get into bed, into the beds of the absent ones; to rest, to gather one's strength.

At dawn, there was nothing left of this melancholy. We felt as though we were on holiday. People were saying:

"Who knows? Perhaps we are being deported for our own good. The front isn't very far off; we shall soon be able to hear the guns. And then the civilian population would be evacuated anyway. . . ."

"Perhaps they were afraid we might help the guerrillas. . . ."

"If you ask me, the whole business of deportation is just a farce. Oh yes, don't laugh. The Boches just want to steal our jewelry. They know we've buried everything, and that they'll have to hunt for it: it's easier when the owners are on holiday. . . ."

On holiday!

These optimistic speeches, which no one believed, helped to pass the time. The few days we lived here went by pleasantly enough, in peace. People were better disposed toward one another. There were no longer any questions of wealth, of social distinction, and importance, only people all condemned to the same fate—still unknown.

Saturday, the day of rest, was chosen for our expulsion.

The night before, we had the traditional Friday evening meal. We said the customary grace for the bread and wine and swallowed our food without a word. We were, we felt, gathered for the last time round the family table. I spent the night turning over thoughts and memories in my mind, unable to find sleep.

At dawn, we were in the street, ready to leave. This time there were no Hungarian police. An agreement had been made with the Jewish Council that they should organize it all themselves.

Our convoy went toward the main synagogue. The town seemed deserted. Yet our friends of yesterday were probably waiting behind their shutters for the moment when they could pillage our houses.

The synagogue was like a huge station: luggage and tears. The altar was broken, the hangings torn down, the walls bare. There were so many of us that we could scarcely breathe. We spent a horrible twenty-four hours there. There were men downstairs; women on the first floor. It was Saturday; it was as though we had come to attend the service. Since no one could go out, people were relieving themselves in a corner.

The following morning, we marched to the station, where a convoy of cattle wagons was waiting. The Hungarian police made us get in—eighty people in each car. We were left a few loaves of bread and some buckets of water. The bars at the window were checked, to see that they were not loose. Then the cars were sealed. In each car one person was placed in charge. If anyone escaped, he would be shot.

Two Gestapo officers strolled about on the platform, smiling: all things considered, everything had gone off very well.

A prolonged whistle split the air. The wheels began to grind. We were on our way.

Lying down was out of the question, and we were only able to sit by deciding to take turns. There was very little air. The lucky ones who happened to be near a window could see the blossoming countryside roll by.

After two days of traveling, we began to be tortured by thirst. Then the heat became unbearable.

Free from all social constraint, the young people gave way openly to instinct, taking advantage of the darkness to copulate in our midst, without caring about anyone else, as though they were alone in the world. The rest pretended not to notice anything.

We still had a few provisions left. But we never ate enough to satisfy our hunger. To save was our rule; to save up for tomorrow. Tomorrow might be worse.

The train stopped at Kaschau, a little town on the Czechoslovak frontier. We realized then that we were not going to stay in Hungary. Our eyes were opened, but too late.

The door of the car slid open. A German officer, accompanied by a Hungarian lieutenant-interpreter, came up and introduced himself.

"From this moment, you come under the authority of the German army. Those of you who still have gold, silver, or watches in your possession must give them up now. Anyone who is later found to have kept anything will be shot on the spot. Secondly, anyone who feels ill may go to the hospital car. That's all."

The Hungarian lieutenant went among us with a basket and collected the last possessions from those who no longer wished to taste the bitterness of terror.

"There are eighty of you in the wagon," added the German officer. "If anyone is missing, you'll all be shot, like dogs. . . ."

They disappeared. The doors were closed. We were caught in a trap, right up to our necks. The doors were nailed up; the way back was finally cut off. The world was a cattle wagon hermetically sealed.

We had a woman with us named Madame Schächter. She was about fifty; her ten-year-old son was with her, crouched in a corner. Her husband and two eldest sons had been deported with the first transport by mistake. The separation had completely broken her.

I knew her well. A quiet woman with tense, burning eyes, she had often been to our house. Her husband, who was a pious man, spent his days and nights in study, and it was she who worked to support the family.

Madame Schächter had gone out of her mind. On the first day of the journey she had already begun to moan and to keep asking why she had been separated from her family. As time went on, her cries grew hysterical.

On the third night, while we slept, some of us sitting one against the other and some standing, a piercing cry split the silence:

"Fire! I can see a fire! I can see a fire!"

There was a moment's panic. Who was it who had cried out? It was Madame Schächter. Standing in the middle of the wagon, in the pale light from the windows, she looked like a withered tree in a cornfield. She pointed her arm toward the window, screaming:

"Look! Look at it! Fire! A terrible fire! Mercy! *Oh, that fire!*"

Some of the men pressed up against the bars. There was nothing there; only the darkness.

The shock of this terrible awakening stayed with us for a long time. We still trembled from it. With every groan of the wheels on the rail, we felt that an abyss was about to open beneath our bodies. Powerless to still our own anguish, we tried to console ourselves:

"She's mad, poor soul. . . ."

Someone had put a damp cloth on her brow, to calm her, but still her screams went on:

"Fire! Fire!"

Her little boy was crying, hanging onto her skirt, trying to take hold of her hands. "It's all right, Mummy! There's nothing there. . . . Sit down. . . ." This shook me even more than his mother's screams had done.

Some women tried to calm her. "You'll find your husband and your sons again . . . in a few days. . . ."

She continued to scream, breathless, her voice broken by sobs. "Jews, listen to me! I can see a fire! There are huge flames! It is a furnace!"

It was as though she were possessed by an evil spirit which spoke from the depths of her being.

We tried to explain it away, more to calm ourselves and to recover our own breath than to comfort her. "She must be very thirsty, poor thing! That's why she keeps talking about a fire devouring her."

But it was in vain. Our terror was about to burst the sides of the train. Our nerves were at breaking point. Our flesh was creeping. It was as though madness were taking possession of us all. We could stand it no longer. Some of the young men forced her to sit down, tied her up, and put a gag in her mouth.

Silence again. The little boy sat down by his mother, crying. I had begun to breathe normally again. We could hear the wheels churning out that monotonous rhythm of a train traveling through the night. We could begin to doze, to rest, to dream. . . .

An hour or two went by like this. Then another scream took our breath away. The woman had broken loose from her bonds and was crying out more loudly than ever:

"Look at the fire! Flames, flames everywhere. . . ."

Once more the young men tied her up and gagged her. They even struck her. People encouraged them:

"Make her be quiet! She's mad! Shut her up! She's not the only one. She can keep her mouth shut. . . ."

They struck her several times on the head—blows that might have killed her. Her little boy clung to her; he did not cry out; he did not say a word. He was not even weeping now.

An endless night. Toward dawn, Madame Schächter calmed down. Crouched in her corner, her bewildered gaze scouring the emptiness, she could no longer see us.

She stayed like that all through the day, dumb, absent, isolated among us. As soon as night fell, she began to scream: "There's a fire over there!" She would point at a spot in space, always the same one. They were tired of hitting her. The heat, the thirst, the pestilential stench, the suffocating lack of air—these were as nothing compared with these screams which tore us to shreds. A few days more and we should all have started to scream too.

But we had reached a station. Those who were next to the windows told us its name:

"Auschwitz."

No one had ever heard that name.

The train did not start up again. The afternoon passed slowly. Then the wagon doors slid open. Two men were allowed to get down to fetch water.

When they came back, they told us that, in exchange for a gold watch, they had discovered that this was the last stop. We would be getting out here. There was a labor camp. Conditions were good. Families would not be split up. Only the young people would go to work in the factories. The old men and invalids would be kept occupied in the fields.

The barometer of confidence soared. Here was a sudden release from the terrors of the previous nights. We gave thanks to God.

Madame Schächter stayed in her corner, wilted, dumb, indifferent to the general confidence. Her little boy stroked her hand.

As dusk fell, darkness gathered inside the wagon. We started to eat our last provisions. At ten in the evening, everyone was looking for a convenient position in which to sleep for a while, and soon we were all asleep. Suddenly:

"The fire! The furnace! Look, over there! . . ."

Waking with a start, we rushed to the window. Yet again we had believed her, even if only for a moment. But there was nothing outside save the darkness of night. With shame in our souls, we went back to our places, gnawed by fear, in spite of ourselves. As she continued to scream, they began to hit her again, and it was with the greatest difficulty that they silenced her.

The man in charge of our wagon called a German officer who was walking about on the platform, and asked him if Madame Schächter could be taken to the hospital car.

"You must be patient," the German replied. "She'll be taken there soon."

Toward eleven o'clock, the train began to move. We pressed against the windows. The convoy was moving slowly. A quarter of an hour later, it slowed down again. Through the windows we could see barbed wire; we realized that this must be the camp.

We had forgotten the existence of Madame Schächter. Suddenly, we heard terrible screams:

"Jews, look! Look through the window! Flames! Look!"

And as the train stopped, we saw this time that flames were gushing out of a tall chimney into the black sky.

Madame Schächter was silent herself. Once more she had become dumb, indifferent, absent, and had gone back to her corner.

We looked at the flames in the darkness. There was an abominable odor floating in the air. Suddenly, our doors opened. Some odd-looking characters, dressed in striped shirts and black trousers leapt into the wagon. They held electric torches and truncheons. They began to strike out to right and left, shouting:

"Everybody get out! Everyone out of the wagon! Quickly!"

We jumped out. I threw a last glance toward Madame Schächter. Her little boy was holding her hand.

In front of us flames. In the air that smell of burning flesh. It must have been about midnight. We had arrived —at Birkenau, reception center for Auschwitz.

The cherished objects we had brought with us thus far were left behind in the train, and with them, at last, our illusions.

Every two yards or so an SS man held his tommy gun trained on us. Hand in hand we followed the crowd.

An SS noncommissioned officer came to meet us, a truncheon in his hand. He gave the order:

"Men to the left! Women to the right!"

Eight words spoken quietly, indifferently, without emotion. Eight short, simple words. Yet that was the moment when I parted from my mother. I had not had time to think, but already I felt the pressure of my father's hand: we were alone. For a part of a second I glimpsed my mother and my sisters moving away to the right. Tzipora held Mother's hand. I saw them disappear into the distance; my mother was stroking my sister's fair hair, as though to protect her, while I walked on with my father and the other men. And I did not know that in that place, at that moment, I was parting from my mother and Tzipora forever. I went on walking. My father held onto my hand.

Behind me, an old man fell to the ground. Near him was an SS man, putting his revolver back in its holster.

My hand shifted on my father's arm. I had one thought —not to lose him. Not to be left alone.

The SS officers gave the order:

"Form fives!"

Commotion. At all costs we must keep together.

"Here, kid, how old are you?"

It was one of the prisoners who asked me this. I could not see his face, but his voice was tense and weary.

"I'm not quite fifteen yet."

"No. Eighteen."

"But I'm not," I said. "Fifteen."

"Fool. Listen to what *I* say."

Then he questioned my father, who replied:

"Fifty."

The other grew more furious than ever.

"No, not fifty. Forty. Do you understand? Eighteen and forty."

He disappeared into the night shadows. A second man came up, spitting oaths at us.

"What have you come here for, you sons of bitches? What are you doing here, eh?"

Someone dared to answer him.

"What do you think? Do you suppose we've come here for our own pleasure? Do you think we asked to come?"

A little more, and the man would have killed him.

"You shut your trap, you filthy swine, or I'll squash you right now! You'd have done better to have hanged yourselves where you were than to come here. Didn't you know what was in store for you at Auschwitz? Haven't you heard about it? In 1944?"

No, we had not heard. No one had told us. He could not believe his ears. His tone of voice became increasingly brutal.

"Do you see that chimney over there? See it? Do you see those flames? (Yes, we did see the flames.) Over there—that's where you're going to be taken. That's your grave, over there. Haven't you realized it yet? You dumb bastards, don't you understand anything? You're going to be burned. Frizzled away. Turned into ashes."

He was growing hysterical in his fury. We stayed motionless, petrified. Surely it was all a nightmare? An unimaginable nightmare?

I heard murmurs around me.

"We've got to do something. We can't let ourselves be killed. We can't go like beasts to the slaughter. We've got to revolt."

There were a few sturdy young fellows among us. They had knives on them, and they tried to incite the others to throw themselves on the armed guards.

One of the young men cried:

"Let the world learn of the existence of Auschwitz. Let everybody hear about it, while they can still escape. . . ."

But the older ones begged their children not to do anything foolish:

"You must never lose faith, even when the sword hangs over your head. That's the teaching of our sages. . . ."

The wind of revolt died down. We continued our march toward the square. In the middle stood the notorious Dr. Mengele (a typical SS officer: a cruel face, but not devoid of intelligence, and wearing a monocle); a conductor's baton in his hand, he was standing among the other officers. The baton moved unremittingly, sometimes to the right, sometimes to the left.

I was already in front of him:

"How old are you?" he asked, in an attempt at a paternal tone of voice.

"Eighteen." My voice was shaking.

"Are you in good health?"

"Yes."

"What's your occupation?"

Should I say that I was a student?

"Farmer," I heard myself say.

This conversation cannot have lasted more than a few seconds. It had seemed like an eternity to me.

The baton moved to the left. I took half a step forward. I wanted to see first where they were sending my father. If he went to the right, I would go after him.

The baton once again pointed to the left for him too. A weight was lifted from my heart.

We did not yet know which was the better side, right or left; which road led to prison and which to the crematory. But for the moment I was happy; I was near my father. Our procession continued to move slowly forward.

Another prisoner came up to us:

"Satisfied?"

"Yes," someone replied.

"Poor devils, you're going to the crematory."

He seemed to be telling the truth. Not far from us, flames were leaping up from a ditch, gigantic flames. They were burning something. A lorry drew up at the pit and delivered its load—little children. Babies! Yes, I saw it—saw it with my own eyes . . . those children in the flames. (Is it surprising that I could not sleep after that? Sleep had fled from my eyes.)

So this was where we were going. A little farther on was another and larger ditch for adults.

I pinched my face. Was I still alive? Was I awake? I could not believe it. How could it be possible for them to burn people, children, and for the world to keep silent? No, none of this could be true. It was a nightmare. . . . Soon I should wake with a start, my heart pounding, and find myself back in the bedroom of my childhood, among my books. . . .

My father's voice drew me from my thoughts:

"It's a shame . . . a shame that you couldn't have gone with your mother. . . . I saw several boys of your age going with their mothers. . . ."

His voice was terribly sad. I realized that he did not want to see what they were going to do to me. He did not want to see the burning of his only son.

My forehead was bathed in cold sweat. But I told him that I did not believe that they could burn people in our age, that humanity would never tolerate it. . . .

"Humanity? Humanity is not concerned with us. Today anything is allowed. Anything is possible, even these crematories. . . ."

His voice was choking.

"Father," I said, "if that is so, I don't want to wait here. I'm going to run to the electric wire. That would be better than slow agony in the flames."

He did not answer. He was weeping. His body was shaken convulsively. Around us, everyone was weeping. Someone began to recite the Kaddish, the prayer for the dead. I do not know if it has ever happened before, in the long history of the Jews, that people have ever recited the prayer for the dead for themselves.

"*Yitgadal veyitkadach shmé raba. . . .* May His Name be blessed and magnified. . . ." whispered my father.

For the first time, I felt revolt rise up in me. Why should I bless His name? The Eternal, Lord of the Universe, the All-Powerful and Terrible, was silent. What had I to thank Him for?

We continued our march. We were gradually drawing closer to the ditch, from which an infernal heat was rising. Still twenty steps to go. If I wanted to bring about my own death, this was the moment. Our line had now only fifteen paces to cover. I bit my lips so that my father would not hear my teeth chattering. Ten steps still. Eight. Seven. We marched slowly on, as though following a hearse at our own funeral. Four steps more. Three steps. There it was now, right in front of us, the pit and its flames. I gathered all that was left of my strength, so that I could break from the ranks and throw myself upon the barbed wire. In the depths of my heart, I bade farewell to my father, to the whole universe; and, in spite of myself, the words formed themselves and issued in a whisper from my lips: *Yitgadal veyitkadach shmé raba*. . . . May His name be blessed and magnified. . . . My heart was bursting. The moment had come. I was face to face with the Angel of Death. . . .

No. Two steps from the pit we were ordered to turn to the left and made to go into a barracks.

I pressed my father's hand. He said:

"Do you remember Madame Schächter, in the train?"

Never shall I forget that night, the first night in camp, which has turned my life into one long night, seven times cursed and seven times sealed. Never shall I forget that smoke. Never shall I forget the little faces of the children, whose bodies I saw turned into wreaths of smoke beneath a silent blue sky.

Never shall I forget those flames which consumed my faith forever.

Never shall I forget that nocturnal silence which deprived me, for all eternity, of the desire to live. Never shall I forget those moments which murdered my God and my soul and turned my dreams to dust. Never shall I forget these things, even if I am condemned to live as long as God Himself. Never.

The barracks we had been made to go into was very long. In the roof were some blue-tinged skylights. The antechamber of Hell must look like this. So many crazed men, so many cries, so much bestial brutality!

There were dozens of prisoners to receive us, truncheons in their hands, striking out anywhere, at anyone, without reason. Orders:

"Strip! Fast! *Los!* Keep only your belts and shoes in your hands. . . ."

We had to throw our clothes at one end of the barracks.

There was already a great heap there. New suits and old, torn coats, rags. For us, this was the true equality: nakedness. Shivering with the cold.

Some SS officers moved about in the room, looking for strong men. If they were so keen on strength, perhaps one should try and pass oneself off as sturdy? My father thought the reverse. It was better not to draw attention to oneself. Our fate would then be the same as the others. (Later, we were to learn that he was right. Those who were selected that day were enlisted in the *Sonder-Kommando*, the unit which worked in the crematories. Bela Katz—son of a big tradesman from our town—had arrived at Birkenau with the first transport, a week before us. When he heard of our arrival, he managed to get word to us that, having been chosen for his strength, he had himself put his father's body into the crematory oven.)

Blows continued to rain down.

"To the barber!"

Belt and shoes in hand, I let myself be dragged off to the barbers. They took our hair off with clippers, and shaved off all the hair on our bodies. The same thought buzzed all the time in my head—not to be separated from my father.

Freed from the hands of the barbers, we began to wander in the crowd, meeting friends and acquaintances. These meetings filled us with joy—yes, joy—"Thank God! You're still alive!"

But others were crying. They used all their remaining strength in weeping. Why had they let themselves be brought here? Why couldn't they have died in their beds? Sobs choked their voices.

Suddenly, someone threw his arms round my neck in an embrace: Yechiel, brother of the rabbi of Sighet. He was sobbing bitterly. I thought he was weeping with joy at still being alive.

"Don't cry, Yechiel," I said. "Don't waste your tears. . . ."

"Not cry? We're on the threshold of death. . . . Soon we shall have crossed over. . . . Don't you understand? How could I not cry?"

Through the blue-tinged skylights I could see the darkness gradually fading. I had ceased to feel fear. And then I was overcome by an inhuman weariness.

Those absent no longer touched even the surface of our memories. We still spoke of them—"Who knows what may have become of them?"—but we had little concern for their fate. We were incapable of thinking of anything at all. Our senses were blunted; everything was blurred as in a fog. It was no longer possible to grasp anything. The instincts of self-preservation, of self-defense, of pride, had all deserted us. In one ultimate moment of lucidity it seemed to me that we were damned souls wandering in the half-world, souls condemned to wander through space till the generations of man came to an end, seeking their redemption, seeking oblivion—without hope of finding it.

Toward five o'clock in the morning, we were driven out of the barracks. The Kapos beat us once more, but I had ceased to feel any pain from their blows. An icy wind enveloped us. We were naked, our shoes and belts in our hands. The command: "Run!" And we ran. After a few minutes of racing, a new barracks.

A barrel of petrol at the entrance. Disinfection. Everyone was soaked in it. Then a hot shower. At high speed. As we came out from the water, we were driven outside. More running. Another barracks, the store. Very long tables. Mountains of prison clothes. On we ran. As we passed, trousers, tunic, shirt, and socks were thrown to us.

Within a few seconds, we had ceased to be men. If the situation had not been tragic, we should have roared with laughter. Such outfits! Meir Katz, a giant, had a child's trousers, and Stern, a thin little chap, a tunic which completely swamped him. We immediately began the necessary exchanges.

I glanced at my father. How he had changed! His eyes had grown dim. I would have liked to speak to him, but I did not know what to say.

The night was gone. The morning star was shining in the sky. I too had become a completely different person. The student of the Talmud, the child that I was, had been consumed in the flames. There remained only a shape that looked like me. A dark flame had entered into my soul and devoured it.

So much had happened within such a few hours that I had lost all sense of time. When had we left our houses? And the ghetto? And the train? Was it only a week? One night—*one single night?*

How long had we been standing like this in the icy wind? An hour? Simply an hour? Sixty minutes?

Surely it was a dream.

Not far from us there were some prisoners at work. Some were digging holes, others carrying sand. None of them so much as glanced at us. We were so many dried-up trees in the heart of a desert. Behind me, some people were talking. I had not the slightest desire to listen to what they were saying, to know who was talking or what they were talking about. No one dared to raise his voice, though there was no supervisor near us. People whispered. Perhaps it was because of the thick smoke which poisoned the air and took one by the throat. . . .

We were made to go into a new barracks, in the "gypsies' camp." In ranks of five.

"And now stay where you are!"

There was no floor. A roof and four walls. Our feet sank into the mud.

Another spell of waiting began. I went to sleep standing up. I dreamed of a bed, of my mother's caress. And I woke up: I was standing, my feet in the mud. Some people collapsed and lay where they were. Others cried:

"Are you mad? We've been told to stay standing. Do you want to bring trouble on us all?"

As if all the trouble in the world had not descended already upon our heads! Gradually, we all sat down in the mud. But we had to jump up constantly, every time a Kapo came in to see if anybody had a pair of new shoes. If so, they had to be given up to him. It was no use opposing this: blows rained down and in the final reckoning you had lost your shoes anyway.

I had new shoes myself. But as they were coated with a thick layer of mud, no one had noticed them. I thanked God, in an improvised prayer, for having created mud in His infinite and wonderful universe.

Suddenly the silence grew oppressive. An SS officer had come in and, with him, the odor of the Angel of Death. We stared fixedly at his fleshy lips. From the middle of the barracks, he harangued us:

"You're in a concentration camp. At Auschwitz. . . ."

A pause. He observed the effect his words had produced. His face has stayed in my memory to this day. A tall man, about thirty, with crime inscribed upon his brow and in the pupils of his eyes. He looked us over as if we were a pack of leprous dogs hanging onto our lives.

"Remember this," he went on. "Remember it forever, Engrave it into your minds. You are at Auschwitz. And Auschwitz is not a convalescent home. It's a concentration camp. Here, you have got to work. If not, you will go straight to the furnace. To the crematory. Work or the crematory—the choice is in your hands."

We had already lived through so much that night, we thought nothing could frighten us any more. But his clipped words made us tremble. Here the word "furnace" was not a word empty of meaning: it floated on the air, mingling with the smoke. It was perhaps the only word which did have any real meaning here. He left the barracks. Kapos appeared, crying:

"All skilled workers—locksmiths, electricians, watchmakers—one step forward!"

The rest of us were made to go to another barracks, a stone one this time. With permission to sit down. A gypsy deportee was in charge of us.

My father was suddenly seized with colic. He got up and went toward the gypsy, asking politely, in German:

"Excuse me, can you tell me where the lavatories are?"

The gypsy looked him up and down slowly, from head to foot. As if he wanted to convince himself that this man addressing him was really a creature of flesh and bone, a living being with a body and a belly. Then, as if he had suddenly woken up from a heavy doze, he dealt my father such a clout that he fell to the ground, crawling back to his place on all fours.

I did not move. What had happened to me? My father had just been struck, before my very eyes, and I had not flickered an eyelid. I had looked on and said nothing. Yesterday, I should have sunk my nails into the criminal's flesh. Had I changed so much, then? So quickly? Now remorse began to gnaw at me. I thought only: I shall never forgive them for that. My father must have guessed my feelings. He whispered in my ear, "It doesn't hurt." His cheek still bore the red mark of the man's hand.

"Everyone outside!"

Ten gypsies had come and joined our supervisor. Whips and truncheons cracked round me. My feet were running without my being aware of it. I tried to hide from the blows behind the others. The spring sunshine.

"Form fives!"

The prisoners whom I had noticed in the morning were working at the side. There was no guard near them, only the shadow of the chimney. . . . Dazed by the sunshine and by my reverie, I felt someone tugging at my sleeve. It was my father. "Come on, my boy."

We marched on. Doors opened and closed again. On we went between the electric wires. At each step, a white placard with a death's head on it stared us in the face. A caption: "Warning. Danger of death." Mockery: was there a single place here where you were not in danger of death?

The gypsies stopped near another barracks. They were replaced by SS, who surrounded us. Revolvers, machine guns, police dogs.

The march had lasted half an hour. Looking around me, I noticed that the barbed wires were behind us. We had left the camp.

It was a beautiful day in May. The fragrance of spring was in the air. The sun was setting in the west.

But we had been marching for only a few moments when we saw the barbed wire of another camp. An iron door with this inscription over it:

"*Work is liberty!*"

Auschwitz.

First impression: this was better than Birkenau. There were two-storied buildings of concrete instead of wooden barracks. There were little gardens here and there. We were led to one of these prison blocks. Seated on the ground by the entrance, we began another session of waiting. Every now and then, someone was made to go in. These were the showers, a compulsory formality at the entrance to all these camps. Even if you were simply passing from one to the other several times a day, you still had to go through the baths every time.

After coming out from the hot water, we stayed shivering in the night air. Our clothes had been left behind in the other block, and we had been promised other outfits.

Toward midnight, we were told to run.

"Faster," shouted our guards. "The faster you run, the sooner you can go to bed."

After a few minutes of this mad race we arrived in front of another block. The prisoner in charge was waiting for us.

He was a young Pole, who smiled at us. He began to talk to us, and, despite our weariness, we listened patiently.

"Comrades, you're in the concentration camp of Auschwitz. There's a long road of suffering ahead of you. But don't lose courage. You've already escaped the gravest danger: selection. So now, muster your strength, and don't lose heart. We shall all see the day of liberation. Have faith in life. Above all else, have faith. Drive out despair, and you will keep death away from yourselves. Hell is not for eternity. And now, a prayer—or rather, a piece of advice: let there be comradeship among you. We are all brothers, and we are all suffering the same fate. The same smoke floats over all our heads. Help one another. It is the only way to survive. Enough said. You're tired. Listen. You're in Block 17. I am responsible for keeping order here. Anyone with a complaint against anyone else can come and see me. That's all. You can go to bed. Two people to a bunk. Good night." The first human words.

No sooner had we climbed into the bunks than we fell into a deep sleep.

The next morning, the "veteran" prisoners treated us without brutality. We went to the wash place. We were given new clothes. We were brought black coffee.

We left the block at about ten o'clock, so that it could be cleaned. Outside the sunshine warmed us. Our morale was much improved. We were feeling the benefit of a night's sleep. Friends met each other, exchanged a few sentences. We talked of everything, except those who had disappeared. The general opinion was that the war was about to end.

At about noon they brought us soup: a plate of thick soup for each person. Tormented though I was by hunger, I refused to touch it. I was still the spoiled child I had always been. My father swallowed my ration.

In the shade of the block, we then had a little siesta. He must have been lying, that SS officer in the muddy barracks. Auschwitz was in fact a rest home. . . .

In the afternoon we were made to line up. Three prisoners brought a table and some medical instruments. With the left sleeve rolled up, each person passed in front of the table. The three "veterans," with needles in their hands, engraved a number on our left arms. I became A-7713. After that I had no other name.

At dusk, roll call. The working units came back. Near the door, the band was playing military marches. Tens of thousands of prisoners stood in rows while the SS checked their numbers.

After roll call, the prisoners from all the blocks scattered to look for friends, relatives, and neighbors who had arrived in the last convoy.

Days passed. In the morning, black coffee. At noon, soup. (By the third day I was eating any kind of soup hungrily.) At six p.m., roll call. Then bread and something. At nine o'clock, bed.

We had already been eight days at Auschwitz. It was during roll call. We were not expecting anything except the sound of the bell which would announce the end of roll call. I suddenly heard someone passing between the rows asking, "Which of you is Wiesel of Sighet?"

The man looking for us was a bespectacled little fellow with a wrinkled, wizened face. My father answered him.

"I'm Wiesel of Sighet."

The little man looked at him for a long while, with his eyes narrowed.

"You don't recognize me—you don't recognize me. I'm a relative of yours. Stein. Have you forgotten me already? Stein! Stein of Antwerp. Reizel's husband. Your wife was Reizel's aunt. She often used to write to us . . . and such letters!"

My father had not recognized him. He must scarcely have known him, since my father was always up to his neck in the affairs of the Jewish community, and much less well versed in family matters. He was always elsewhere, lost in his thoughts. (Once a cousin came to see us at Sighet. She had been staying with us and eating at our table for over a fortnight before my father noticed her presence for the first time.) No, he could not have remembered Stein. As for me, I recognized him at once. I had known his wife Reizel before she left for Belgium.

He said, "I was deported in 1942. I heard that a transport had come in from your region, and I came to find you. I thought perhaps you might have news of Reizel and my little boys. They stayed behind in Antwerp. . . ."

I knew nothing about them. Since 1940, my mother had not had a single letter from them. But I lied.

"Yes, my mother's had news from your family. Reizel is very well. The children too. . . ."

He wept with joy. He would have liked to stay longer, to learn more details, to drink in the good news, but an SS came up, and he had to go, calling to us that he would be back the next day.

The bell gave us the signal to disperse. We went to get our evening meal of bread and margarine. I was dreadfully hungry and swallowed my ration on the spot.

My father said, "You don't want to eat it all at once. Tomorrow's another day. . . ."

And seeing that his advice had come too late and that there was nothing left of my ration, he did not even begin his own.

"Personally, I'm not hungry," he said.

We stayed at Auschwitz for three weeks. We had nothing to do. We slept a great deal in the afternoon and at night.

The only worry was to avoid moves, to stay here as long as possible. It was not difficult; it was simply a matter of never putting oneself down as a skilled worker. Laborers were being kept till the end.

At the beginning of the third week, the prisoner in charge of our block was deprived of his office, being considered too humane. Our new head was savage, and his assistants were real monsters. The good days were over.

We began to wonder if it would not be better to let oneself be chosen for the next move.

Stein, our relation from Antwerp, continued to visit us, and from time to time he would bring a half ration of bread.

"Here, this is for you, Eliezer."

Every time he came, there would be tears running down his face, congealing there, freezing. He would often say to my father:

"Take care of your son. He's very weak and dried up. Look after him well, to avoid the selection. Eat! It doesn't matter what or when. Eat everything you can. The weak don't hang about for long here. . . ."

And he was so thin himself, so dried up, so weak. . . .

"The only thing that keeps me alive," he used to say, "is that Reizel and the children are still alive. If it wasn't for them, I couldn't keep going."

He came toward us one evening, his face radiant.

"A transport's just come in from Antwerp. I'm going to see them tomorrow. They'll be sure to have news."

He went off.

We were not to see him again. He had had news. Real news.

In the evening, lying on our beds, we would try to sing some of the Hasidic melodies, and Akiba Drumer would break our hearts with his deep, solemn voice.

Some talked of God, of his mysterious ways, of the sins of the Jewish people, and of their future deliverance. But I had ceased to pray. How I sympathized with Job! I did not deny God's existence, but I doubted His absolute justice.

Akiba Drumer said: "God is testing us. He wants to find out whether we can dominate our base instincts and kill the Satan within us. We have no right to despair. And if he punishes us relentlessly, it's a sign that He loves us all the more."

Hersch Genud, well versed in the cabbala, spoke of the end of the world and the coming of Messiah.

Only occasionally during these conversations did the thought occur to me: "Where is my mother at this moment? And Tzipora . . .?"

"Your mother is still a young woman," said my father on one occasion. "She must be in a labor camp. And Tzipora's a big girl now, isn't she? She must be in a camp, too."

How we should have liked to believe it. We pretended, for what if the other one should still be believing it?

All the skilled workers had already been sent to other camps. There were only about a hundred of us ordinary laborers left.

"It's your turn today," said the secretary of the block. "You're going with the next transport."

At ten o'clock we were given our daily ration of bread. We were surrounded by about ten SS. On the door the plaque: "*Work is liberty.*" We were counted. And then, there we were, right out in the country on the sunny road. In the sky a few little white clouds.

We walked slowly. The guards were in no hurry. We were glad of this. As we went through the villages, many of the Germans stared at us without surprise. They had probably already seen quite a few of these processions.

On the way, we met some young German girls. The guards began to tease them. The girls giggled, pleased. They let themselves be kissed and tickled, exploding with laughter. They were all laughing and joking and shouting blandishments at one another for a good part of the way. During this time, at least we did not have to endure either shouts or blows from the rifle butt.

At the end of four hours, we reached our new camp: Buna. The iron gate closed behind us.

The camp looked as though it had suffered an epidemic: empty and dead. There were just a few well-clad prisoners walking about between the blocks.

Of course, we had to go through the showers first. The head of our camp joined us there. He was a strong, well-built, broad-shouldered man: bull neck, thick lips, frizzled hair. He looked kind. A smile shone from time to time in his gray-blue eyes. Our convoy included a few children ten and twelve years old. The officer took an interest in them and gave orders for them to be brought food.

After we had been given new clothes, we were installed in two tents. We had to wait to be enlisted in the labor units, then we could pass into the block.

That evening, the labor units came back from the work yards. Roll call. We began to look for familiar faces, to seek information, to question the veteran prisoners about which labor unit was the best, which block one should try to get into. The prisoners all agreed, saying, "Buna's a very good camp. You can stand it. The important thing is not to get transferred to the building unit. . . ."

As if the choice were in our own hands.

The head of our tent was a German. An assassin's face, fleshy lips, hands like a wolf's paws. He was so fat he could hardly move. Like the leader of the camp, he loved children. As soon as we arrived, he had brought them bread, soup, and margarine. (Actually, this was not disinterested affection: there was a considerable traffic in children among homosexuals here, I learned later.)

The head told us: "You're staying here three days in quarantine. Then you're going to work. Tomorrow, medical inspection."

One of his assistants—a hard-faced boy, with hooligan's eyes—came up to me:

"Do you want to get into a good unit?"

"I certainly do. But on one condition: I want to stay with my father."

"All right," he said. "I can arrange that. For a small consideration: your shoes. I'll give you some others."

I refused to give him my shoes. They were all I had left.

"I'll give you an extra ration of bread and margarine."

He was very keen on my shoes; but I did not give them up to him. (Later on they were taken from me just the same. But in exchange for nothing this time.)

Medical examination in the open air in the early hours of the morning, before three doctors seated on a bench.

The first barely examined me at all. He was content merely to ask:

"Are you in good health?"

Who would have dared say anything to the contrary?

The dentist, on the other hand, seemed most conscientious: he would order us to open our mouths wide. Actually he was not looking for decayed teeth, but gold ones. Anyone who had gold in his mouth had his number added to a list. I myself had a gold crown.

The first three days passed by rapidly. On the fourth day, at dawn, when we were standing in front of the tent, the Kapos appeared. Then each began to choose the men who suited him:

"You . . . you . . . you and you. . . ." They pointed a finger, as though choosing cattle or merchandise.

We followed our Kapo, a young man. He made us stop at the entrance to the first block, near the door of the camp. This was the orchestra block. "Go in," he ordered. We were surprised. What had we to do with music?

The band played a military march, always the same one. Dozens of units left for the workyards, in step. The Kapos beat time: "Left, right, left, right."

Some SS officers, pen and paper in hand, counted the men as they went out. The band went on playing the same march until the last unit had gone by. Then the conductor's baton was still. The band stopped dead, and the Kapos yelled:

"Form fives!"

We left the camp without music, but in step: we still had the sound of the march in our ears.

"Left, right! Left, right!"

We started talking to the musicians next to us.

We drew up in ranks of five, with the musicians. They were nearly all Jews: Juliek, a bespectacled Pole with a cynical smile on his pale face; Louis, a distinguished violinist who came from Holland—he complained that they would not let him play Beethoven: Jews were not allowed to play German music; Hans, a lively young Berliner. The foreman was a Pole, Franek, a former student from Warsaw.

Juliek explained to me: "We work in a warehouse for electrical equipment, not far from here. The work isn't in the least difficult or dangerous. But Idek, the Kapo, has bouts of madness now and then, when it's best to keep out of his way."

"You're lucky, son," smiled Hans. "You've landed in a good unit. . . ."

Ten minutes later, we were in front of the warehouse. A German employee, a civilian, the *meister*, came to meet us. He paid us about as much attention as a dealer might who was just receiving a delivery of old rags.

Our comrades had been right; the work was not difficult. Sitting on the ground, we had to count bolts, bulbs, and small electrical fittings. The Kapo explained to us at great length the vast importance of our work, warning us that anyone found slacking would have him to reckon with. My new comrades reassured me.

"There's nothing to be scared of. He has to say that because of the *meister*."

There were a number of Polish civilians there, and a few French women, who were casting friendly glances at the musicians.

Franek, the foreman, put me in a corner. "Don't kill yourself; there's no hurry. But mind an SS man doesn't catch you unawares."

"Please . . . I would have liked to be by my father."

"All right. Your father'll be working here by your side."

We were lucky.

There were two boys attached to our group: Yossi and Tibi, two brothers. They were Czechs whose parents had been exterminated at Birkenau. They lived, body and soul, for each other.

They and I very soon became friends. Having once belonged to a Zionist youth organization, they knew innumerable Hebrew chants. Thus we would often hum tunes evoking the calm waters of Jordan and the majestic sanctity of Jerusalem. And we would often talk of Palestine. Their parents, like mine, had lacked the courage to wind up their affairs and emigrate while there was still time. We decided that, if we were granted our lives until the liberation, we would not stay in Europe a day longer. We would take the first boat for Haifa.

Still lost in his cabbalistic dreams, Akiba Drumer had discovered a verse in the Bible which, interpreted in terms of numerology, enabled him to predict that the deliverance was due within the coming weeks.

We had left the tents for the musicians' block. We were entitled to a blanket, a wash bowl, and a bar of soap. The head of the block was a German Jew.

It was good to be under a Jew. He was called Alphonse. A young man with an extraordinarily aged face, he was entirely devoted to the cause of "his" block. Whenever he could, he would organize a cauldron of soup for the young ones, the weak, all those who were dreaming more about an extra plateful than of liberty.

One day when we had just come back from the warehouse, I was sent for by the secretary of the block.

"A-7713?"

"That's me."

"After eating, you're to go to the dentist."

"But I haven't got toothache."

"After eating. Without fail."

I went to the hospital block. There were about twenty prisoners waiting in a queue in front of the door. It did not take long to discover why we had been summoned: it was for the extraction of our gold teeth.

The dentist, a Jew from Czechoslovakia, had a face like a death mask. When he opened his mouth, there was a horrible sight of yellow, decaying teeth. I sat in the chair and asked him humbly: "Please, what are you going to do?"

"Simply take out your gold crown," he replied, indifferently.

I had the idea of pretending to be ill.

"You couldn't wait a few days, Doctor? I don't feel very well. I've got a temperature. . . ."

He wrinkled his brow, thought for a moment, and took my pulse.

"All right, son. When you feel better, come back and see me. But don't wait till I send for you!"

I went to see him a week later. With the same excuse: I still did not feel any better. He did not seem to show any surprise, and I do not know if he believed me. He was probably glad to see that I had come back of my own accord, as I had promised. He gave me another reprieve.

A few days after this visit of mine, they closed the dentist's surgery, and he was thrown into prison. He was going to be hanged. It was alleged that he had been running a private traffic of his own in the prisoners' gold teeth. I did not feel any pity for him. I was even pleased about what had happened. I had saved my gold crown. It might be useful to me one day to buy something—bread or life. I now took little interest in anything except my daily plate of soup and my crust of stale bread. Bread, soup—these were my whole life. I was a body. Perhaps less than that even: a starved stomach. The stomach alone was aware of the passage of time.

At the warehouse I often worked next to a young French girl. We did not speak to one another, since she knew no German and I did not understand French.

She seemed to me to be a Jewess, though here she passed as Aryan. She was a forced labor deportee.

One day when Idek was seized with one of his fits of frenzy, I got in his way. He leapt on me, like a wild animal, hitting me in the chest, on the head, throwing me down and pulling me up again, his blows growing more and more violent, until I was covered with blood. As I was biting my lips to stop myself from screaming with pain, he must have taken my silence for defiance, for he went on hitting me even harder.

Suddenly he calmed down. As if nothing had happened, he sent me back to work. It was as though we had been taking part together in some game where we each had our role to play.

I dragged myself to my corner. I ached all over. I felt

a cool hand wiping my blood-stained forehead. It was the French girl. She gave me her mournful smile and slipped a bit of bread into my hand. She looked into my eyes. I felt that she wanted to say something but was choked by fear. For a long moment she stayed like that, then her face cleared and she said to me in almost perfect German:

"Bite your lip, little brother. . . . Don't cry. Keep your anger and hatred for another day, for later on. The day will come, but not now. . . . Wait. Grit your teeth and wait. . . ."

Many years later, in Paris, I was reading my paper in the Metro. Facing me was a very beautiful woman with black hair and dreamy eyes. I had seen those eyes before somewhere. It was she.

"You don't recognize me?"

"I don't know you."

"In 1944 you were in Germany, at Buna, weren't you?"

"Yes. . . ."

"You used to work in the electrical warehouse. . . ."

"Yes," she said, somewhat disturbed. And then, after a moment's silence: "Wait a minute . . . I do remember. . . ."

"Idek, the Kapo . . . the little Jewish boy . . . your kind words. . . ."

We left the Metro together to sit down on the terrace of a café. We spent the whole evening reminiscing.

Before I parted from her, I asked her: "May I ask you a question?"

"I know what it will be—go on."

"What?"

"Am I Jewish . . . ? Yes, I am Jewish. From a religious family. During the occupation I obtained forged papers and passed myself off as an Aryan. That's how I was enlisted in the forced labor groups, and when I was deported to Germany, I escaped the concentration camp. At the warehouse, no one knew I could speak German. That would have aroused suspicions. Saying those few words to you was risky: but I knew you wouldn't give me away. . . ."

Another time we had to load Diesel engines onto trains supervised by German soldiers. Idek's nerves were on edge. He was restraining himself with great difficulty. Suddenly, his frenzy broke out. The victim was my father.

"You lazy old devil!" Idek began to yell. "Do you call that work?"

And he began to beat him with an iron bar. At first my father crouched under the blows, then he broke in two, like a dry tree struck by lightning, and collapsed.

I had watched the whole scene without moving. I kept quiet. In fact I was thinking of how to get farther away so that I would not be hit myself. What is more, any anger I felt at that moment was directed, not against the Kapo, but against my father. I was angry with him, for not knowing how to avoid Idek's outbreak. That is what concentration camp life had made of me.

Franek, the foreman, one day noticed the gold-crowned tooth in my mouth.

"Give me your crown, kid."

I told him it was impossible, that I could not eat without it.

"What do they give you to eat, anyway?"

I found another answer; the crown had been put down on a list after the medical inspection. This could bring trouble on us both.

"If you don't give me your crown, you'll pay for it even more."

This sympathetic, intelligent youth was suddenly no longer the same person. His eyes gleamed with desire. I told him I had to ask my father's advice.

"Ask your father, kid. But I want an answer by tomorrow."

When I spoke to my father about it, he turned pale, was silent a long while, and then said:

"No, son, you mustn't do it."

"He'll take it out on us!"

"He won't dare."

But alas, Franek knew where to touch me; he knew my weak point. My father had never done military service, and he never succeeded in marching in step. Here, every time we moved from one place to another in a body, we marched in strict rhythm. This was Franek's chance to torment my father and to thrash him savagely every day. Left, right: punch! Left, right: clout!

I decided to give my father lessons myself, to teach him to change step, and to keep to the rhythm. We began to do exercises in front of our block. I would give the commands: "Left, right!" and my father would practice. Some of the prisoners began to laugh at us.

"Look at this little officer teaching the old chap to march. . . . Hey, general, how many rations of bread does the old boy give you for this?"

But my father's progress was still inadequate, and blows continued to rain down on him.

"So you still can't march in step, you lazy old devil?"

These scenes were repeated for two weeks. We could not stand any more. We had to give in. When the day came, Franek burst into wild laughter.

"I knew it, I knew quite well I would win. Better late than never. And because you've made me wait, that's going to cost you a ration of bread. A ration of bread for one of my pals, a famous dentist from Warsaw, so that he can take your crown out."

"What? *My* ration of bread so that you can have *my* crown?"

Franek grinned.

"What would you like then? Shall I break your teeth with my fist?"

That same evening, in the lavatory the dentist from Warsaw pulled out my crowned tooth, with the aid of a rusty spoon.

Franek grew kinder. Occasionally, he even gave me

extra soup. But that did not last long. A fortnight later, all the Poles were transferred to another camp. I had lost my crown for nothing.

A few days before the Poles left, I had a new experience.

It was a Sunday morning. Our unit did not need to go to work that day. But all the same Idek would not hear of our staying in the camp. We had to go to the warehouse. This sudden enthusiasm for work left us stunned.

At the warehouse, Idek handed us over to Franek, saying, "Do what you like. But do something. If not, you'll hear from me. . . ."

And he disappeared.

We did not know what to do. Tired of squatting down, we each in turn went for a walk through the warehouse, looking for a bit of bread some civilian might have left behind.

When I came to the back of the building, I heard a noise coming from a little room next door. I went up and saw Idek with a young Polish girl, half-naked, on a mattress. Then I understood why Idek had refused to let us stay in the camp. Moving a hundred prisoners so that he could lie with a girl! It struck me as so funny that I burst out laughing.

Idek leapt up, turned around, and saw me, while the girl tried to cover up her breasts. I wanted to run away, but my legs were glued to the ground. Idek seized me by the throat.

Speaking in a low voice, he said, "You wait and see, kid. . . . You'll soon find out what leaving your work's going to cost you. . . . You're going to pay for this pretty soon. . . . And now, go back to your place."

Half an hour before work usually ended, the Kapo collected together the whole unit. Roll call. Nobody knew what had happened. Roll call at this time of day? Here? But I knew. The Kapo gave a short speech.

"An ordinary prisoner has no right to meddle in other people's affairs. One of you does not seem to have understood this. I'm obliged, therefore, to make it very clear to him once and for all."

I felt the sweat run down my back.

"A-7713!"

I came forward.

"A box!" he ordered.

They brought him a box.

"Lie down on it! On your stomach!"

I obeyed.

Then I was aware of nothing but the strokes of the whip.

"One . . . two . . .," he counted.

He took his time between each stroke. Only the first ones really hurt me. I could hear him counting:

"Ten . . . eleven . . ."

His voice was calm and reached me as through a thick wall.

"Twenty-three . . ."

Two more, I thought, half conscious. The Kapo waited.

"Twenty-four . . . twenty-five!"

It was over. But I did not realize it, for I had fainted. I felt myself come round as a bucket of cold water was thrown over me. I was still lying on the box. I could just vaguely make out the wet ground surrounding me. Then I heard someone cry out. It must have been the Kapo. I began to distinguish the words he was shouting.

"Get up!"

I probably made some movement to raise myself, because I felt myself falling back onto the box. How I longed to get up!

"Get up!" he yelled more loudly.

If only I could have answered him, at least; if only I could have told him that I could not move! But I could not manage to open my lips.

At Idek's command, two prisoners lifted me up and led me in front of him.

"Look me in the eye!"

I looked at him without seeing him. I was thinking of my father. He must have suffered more than I did.

"Listen to me, you bastard!" said Idek, coldly. "That's for your curiosity. You'll get five times more if you dare tell anyone what you saw! Understand?"

I nodded my head, once, ten times. I nodded ceaselessly. as if my head had decided to say yes without ever stopping.

One Sunday, when half of us—including my father—were at work, the rest—including myself—were in the block, taking advantage of the chance to stay in bed late in the morning.

At about ten o'clock, the air-raid sirens began to wail. An alert. The leaders of the block ran to assemble us inside, while the SS took refuge in the shelters. As it was relatively easy to escape during a warning—the guards left their look-out posts and the electric current was cut off in the barbed-wire fences—the SS had orders to kill anyone found outside the blocks.

Within a few minutes, the camp looked like an abandoned ship. Not a living soul on the paths. Near the kitchen, two cauldrons of steaming hot soup had been left, half full. Two cauldrons of soup, right in the middle of the path, with no one guarding them! A feast for kings, abandoned, supreme temptation! Hundreds of eyes looked at them, sparkling with desire. Two lambs, with a hundred wolves lying in wait for them. Two lambs without a shepherd—a gift. But who would dare?

Terror was stronger than hunger. Suddenly, we saw the door of Block 37 open imperceptibly. A man appeared, crawling like a worm in the direction of the cauldrons.

Hundreds of eyes followed his movements. Hundreds of men crawled with him, scraping their knees with his on the gravel. Every heart trembled, but with envy above all. This man had dared.

He reached the first cauldron. Hearts raced: he had

succeeded. Jealousy consumed us, burned us up like straw. We never thought for a moment of admiring him. Poor hero, committing suicide for a ration of soup! In our thoughts we were murdering him.

Stretched out by the cauldron, he was now trying to raise himself up to the edge. Either from weakness or fear he stayed there, trying, no doubt, to muster up the last of his strength. At last he succeeded in hoisting himself onto the edge of the pot. For a moment, he seemed to be looking at himself, seeking his ghostlike reflection in the soup. Then, for no apparent reason, he let out a terrible cry, a rattle such as I had never heard before, and, his mouth open, thrust his head toward the still steaming liquid. We jumped at the explosion. Falling back onto the ground, his face stained with soup, the man writhed for a few seconds at the foot of the cauldron, then he moved no more.

Then we began to hear the airplanes. Almost at once, the barracks began to shake.

"They're bombing Buna!" someone shouted.

I thought of my father. But I was glad all the same. To see the whole works go up in fire—what revenge! We had heard so much talk about the defeats of German troops on various fronts, but we did not know how much to believe. This, today, was real!

We were not afraid. And yet, if a bomb had fallen on the blocks, it alone would have claimed hundreds of victims on the spot. But we were no longer afraid of death; at any rate, not of that death. Every bomb that exploded filled us with joy and gave us new confidence in life.

The raid lasted over an hour. If it could only have lasted ten times ten hours! . . . Then silence fell once more. The last sound of an American plane was lost on the wind, and we found ourselves back again in the cemetery. A great trail of black smoke was rising up on the horizon. The sirens began to wail once more. It was the end of the alert.

Everyone came out of the blocks. We filled our lungs with the fire- and smoke-laden air, and our eyes shone with hope. A bomb had fallen in the middle of the camp, near the assembly point, but it had not gone off. We had to take it outside the camp.

The head of the camp, accompanied by his assistant and the chief Kapo, made a tour of inspection along the paths. The raid had left traces of terror on his face.

Right in the middle of the camp lay the body of the man with the soup-stained face, the only victim. The cauldrons were taken back into the kitchen.

The SS had gone back to their lookout posts, behind their machine guns. The interlude was over.

At the end of an hour, we saw the units come back, in step, as usual. Joyfully, I caught sight of my father.

"Several buildings have been flattened right out," he said, "but the warehouse hasn't suffered."

In the afternoon we went cheerfully to clear away the ruins.

A week later, on the way back from work, we noticed in the center of the camp, at the assembly place, a black gallows.

We were told that soup would not be distributed until after roll call. This took longer than usual. The orders were given in a sharper manner than on other days, and in the air there were strange undertones.

"Bare your heads!" yelled the head of the camp, suddenly.

Ten thousand caps were simultaneously removed.

"Cover your heads!"

Ten thousand caps went back onto their skulls, as quick as lightning.

The gate to the camp opened. An SS section appeared and surrounded us: one SS at every three paces. On the lookout towers the machine guns were trained on the assembly place.

"They fear trouble," whispered Juliek.

Two SS men had gone to the cells. They came back with

the condemned man between them. He was a youth from Warsaw. He had three years of concentration camp life behind him. He was a strong, well-built boy, a giant in comparison with me.

His back to the gallows, his face turned toward his judge, who was the head of the camp, the boy was pale, but seemed more moved than afraid. His manacled hands did not tremble. His eyes gazed coldly at the hundreds of SS guards, the thousands of prisoners who surrounded him.

The head of the camp began to read his verdict, hammering out each phrase:

"In the name of Himmler . . . prisoner Number . . . stole during the alert. . . . According to the law . . . paragraph . . . prisoner Number . . . is condemned to death. May this be a warning and an example to all prisoners."

No one moved.

I could hear my heart beating. The thousands who had died daily at Auschwitz and at Birkenau in the crematory ovens no longer troubled me. But this one, leaning against his gallows—he overwhelmed me.

"Do you think this ceremony'll be over soon? I'm hungry. . . . " whispered Juliek.

At a sign from the head of the camp, the Lagerkapo advanced toward the condemned man. Two prisoners helped him in his task—for two plates of soup.

The Kapo wanted to bandage the victim's eyes, but he refused.

After a long moment of waiting, the executioner put the rope round his neck. He was on the point of motioning to his assistants to draw the chair away from the prisoner's feet, when the latter cried, in a calm, strong voice:

"Long live liberty! A curse upon Germany! A curse . . .! A cur—"

The executioners had completed their task.

A command cleft the air like a sword.

"Bare your heads."

Ten thousand prisoners paid their last respects.

"Cover your heads!"

Then the whole camp, block after block, had to march past the hanged man and stare at the dimmed eyes, the lolling tongue of death. The Kapos and heads of each block forced everyone to look him full in the face.

After the march, we were given permission to return to the blocks for our meal.

I remember that I found the soup excellent that evening. . . .

I witnessed other hangings. I never saw a single one of the victims weep. For a long time those dried-up bodies had forgotten the bitter taste of tears.

Except once. The Oberkapo of the fifty-second cable unit was a Dutchman, a giant, well over six feet. Seven hundred prisoners worked under his orders, and they all loved him like a brother. No one had ever received a blow at his hands, nor an insult from his lips.

He had a young boy under him, a *pipel*, as they were called—a child with a refined and beautiful face, unheard of in this camp.

(At Buna, the *pipel* were loathed; they were often crueller than adults. I once saw one of thirteen beating his father because the latter had not made his bed properly. The old man was crying softly while the boy shouted: "If you don't stop crying at once I shan't bring you any more bread. Do you understand?" But the Dutchman's little servant was loved by all. He had the face of a sad angel.)

One day, the electric power station at Buna was blown up. The Gestapo, summoned to the spot, suspected sabotage. They found a trail. It eventually led to the Dutch Oberkapo. And there, after a search, they found an important stock of arms.

The Oberkapo was arrested immediately. He was tortured for a period of weeks, but in vain. He would not give a single name. He was transferred to Auschwitz. We never heard of him again.

But his little servant had been left behind in the camp in prison. Also put to torture, he too would not speak. Then the SS sentenced him to death, with two other prisoners who had been discovered with arms.

One day when we came back from work, we saw three gallows rearing up in the assembly place, three black crows. Roll call. SS all round us, machine guns trained: the traditional ceremony. Three victims in chains—and one of them, the little servant, the sad-eyed angel.

The SS seemed more preoccupied, more disturbed than usual. To hang a young boy in front of thousands of spectators was no light matter. The head of the camp read the verdict. All eyes were on the child. He was lividly pale, almost calm, biting his lips. The gallows threw its shadow over him.

This time the Lagerkapo refused to act as executioner. Three SS replaced him.

The three victims mounted together onto the chairs.

The three necks were placed at the same moment within the nooses.

"Long live liberty!" cried the two adults.

But the child was silent.

"Where is God? Where is He?" someone behind me asked.

At a sign from the head of the camp, the three chairs tipped over.

Total silence throughout the camp. On the horizon, the sun was setting.

"Bare your heads!" yelled the head of the camp. His voice was raucous. We were weeping.

"Cover your heads!"

Then the march past began. The two adults were no longer alive. Their tongues hung swollen, blue-tinged. But the third rope was still moving; being so light, the child was still alive. . . .

For more than half an hour he stayed there, struggling between life and death, dying in slow agony under our eyes.

And we had to look him full in the face. He was still alive when I passed in front of him. His tongue was still red, his eyes were not yet glazed.

Behind me, I heard the same man asking:

"Where is God now?"

And I heard a voice within me answer him:

"Where is He? Here He is—He is hanging here on this gallows. . . ."

That night the soup tasted of corpses.

The summer was coming to an end. The Jewish year was nearly over.

On the eve of Rosh Hashanah, the last day of that accursed year, the whole camp was electric with the tension which was in all our hearts. In spite of everything, this day was different from any other. The last day of the year. The word "last" rang very strangely. What if it were indeed the last day?

They gave us our evening meal, a very thick soup, but no one touched it. We wanted to wait until after prayers. At the place of assembly, surrounded by the electrified barbed wire, thousands of silent Jews gathered, their faces stricken.

Night was falling. Other prisoners continued to crowd in, from every block, able suddenly to conquer time and space and submit both to their will.

"What are You, my God," I thought angrily, "compared to this afflicted crowd, proclaiming to You their faith, their anger, their revolt? What does Your greatness mean, Lord of the Universe, in the face of all this weakness, this decomposition, and this decay? Why do You still trouble their sick minds, their crippled bodies?"

Ten thousand men had come to attend the solemn service, heads of the blocks, Kapos, functionaries of death.

"Bless the Eternal. . . ."

The voice of the officiant had just made itself heard. I thought at first it was the wind.

"Blessed be the Name of the Eternal!"

Thousands of voices repeated the benediction; thousands of men prostrated themselves like trees before a tempest.

"Blessed be the Name of the Eternal!"

Why, but why should I bless Him? In every fiber I rebelled. Because He had had thousands of children burned in His pits? Because He kept six crematories working night and day, on Sundays and feast days? Because in His great might He had created Auschwitz, Birkenau, Buna, and so many factories of death? How could I say to Him: "Blessed art Thou, Eternal, Master of the Universe, Who chose us from among the races to be tortured day and night, to see our fathers, our mothers, our brothers, end in the crematory? Praised be Thy Holy Name, Thou Who hast chosen us to be butchered on Thine altar?"

I heard the voice of the officiant rising up, powerful yet at the same time broken, amid the tears, the sobs, the sighs of the whole congregation:

"All the earth and the Universe are God's!"

He kept stopping every moment, as though he did not have the strength to find the meaning beneath the words. The melody choked in his throat.

And I, mystic that I had been, I thought:

"Yes, man is very strong, greater than God. When You were deceived by Adam and Eve, You drove them out of Paradise. When Noah's generation displeased You, You brought down the Flood. When Sodom no longer found favor in Your eyes, You made the sky rain down fire and sulphur. But these men here, whom You have betrayed, whom You have allowed to be tortured, butchered, gassed, burned, what do they do? They pray before You! They praise Your name!"

"All creation bears witness to the Greatness of God!"

Once, New Year's Day had dominated my life. I knew that my sins grieved the Eternal; I implored his forgiveness. Once, I had believed profoundly that upon one solitary deed of mine, one solitary prayer, depended the salvation of the world.

This day I had ceased to plead. I was no longer capable of lamentation. On the contrary, I felt very strong. I was the accuser, God the accused. My eyes were open and I was alone—terribly alone in a world without God and without man. Without love or mercy. I had ceased to be anything but ashes, yet I felt myself to be stronger than the Almighty, to whom my life had been tied for so long. I stood amid that praying congregation, observing it like a stranger.

The service ended with the Kaddish. Everyone recited the Kaddish over his parents, over his children, over his brothers, and over himself.

We stayed for a long time at the assembly place. No one dared to drag himself away from this mirage. Then it was time to go to bed and slowly the prisoners made their way over to their blocks. I heard people wishing one another a Happy New Year!

I ran off to look for my father. And at the same time I was afraid of having to wish him a Happy New Year when I no longer believed in it.

He was standing near the wall, bowed down, his shoulders sagging as though beneath a heavy burden. I went up to him, took his hand and kissed it. A tear fell upon it. Whose was that tear? Mine? His? I said nothing. Nor did he. We had never understood one another so clearly.

The sound of the bell jolted us back to reality. We must go to bed. We came back from far away. I raised my eyes to look at my father's face leaning over mine, to try to discover a smile or something resembling one upon the aged, dried-up countenance. Nothing. Not the shadow of an expression. Beaten.

Yom Kippur. The Day of Atonement.

Should we fast? The question was hotly debated. To fast would mean a surer, swifter death. We fasted here the whole year round. The whole year was Yom Kippur. But others said that we should fast simply because it was dangerous to do so. We should show God that even here, in this enclosed hell, we were capable of singing His praises.

I did not fast, mainly to please my father, who had forbidden me to do so. But further, there was no longer any reason why I should fast. I no longer accepted God's silence. As I swallowed my bowl of soup, I saw in the gesture an act of rebellion and protest against Him.

And I nibbled my crust of bread.

In the depths of my heart, I felt a great void.

The SS gave us a fine New Year's gift.

We had just come back from work. As soon as we had passed through the door of the camp, we sensed something different in the air. Roll call did not take so long as usual. The evening soup was given out with great speed and swallowed down at once in anguish.

I was no longer in the same block as my father. I had been transferred to another unit, the building one, where, twelve hours a day, I had to drag heavy blocks of stone about. The head of my new block was a German Jew, small of stature, with piercing eyes. He told us that evening that no one would be allowed to go out after the evening soup. And soon a terrible word was circulating—selection.

We knew what that meant. An SS man would examine us. Whenever he found a weak one, a *musulman* as we called them, he would write his number down: good for the crematory.

After soup, we gathered together between the beds. The veterans said:

"You're lucky to have been brought here so late. This camp is paradise today, compared with what it was like two years ago. Buna was a real hell then. There was no water, no blankets, less soup and bread. At night we slept almost naked, and it was below thirty degrees. The corpses were collected in hundreds every day. The work was hard. Today, this is a little paradise. The Kapos had orders to kill a certain number of prisoners every day. And every week—selection. A merciless selection. . . . Yes, you're lucky."

"Stop it! Be quiet!" I begged. "You can tell your stories tomorrow or on some other day."

They burst out laughing. They were not veterans for nothing.

"Are you scared? So were we scared. And there was plenty to be scared of in those days."

The old men stayed in their corner, dumb, motionless, hunted. Some were praying.

An hour's delay. In an hour, we should know the verdict—death or a reprieve.

And my father? Suddenly I remembered him. How would he pass the selection? He had aged so much. . . .

The head of our block had never been outside concentration camps since 1933. He had already been through all the slaughterhouses, all the factories of death. At about nine o'clock, he took up his position in our midst:

"Achtung!"

There was instant silence.

"Listen carefully to what I am going to say." (For the first time, I heard his voice quiver.) "In a few moments the selection will begin. You must get completely undressed. Then one by one you go before the SS doctors. I hope you will all succeed in getting through. But you must help your own chances. Before you go into the next room, move about in some way so that you give yourselves a little color. Don't walk slowly, run! Run as if the devil were after you! Don't look at the SS. Run, straight in front of you!"

He broke off for a moment, then added:

"And, the essential thing, don't be afraid!"

Here was a piece of advice we should have liked very much to be able to follow.

I got undressed, leaving my clothes on the bed. There was no danger of anyone stealing them this evening.

Tibi and Yossi, who had changed their unit at the same time as I had, came up to me and said:

"Let's keep together. We shall be stronger."

Yossi was murmuring something between his teeth. He must have been praying. I had never realized that Yossi was a believer. I had even always thought the reverse. Tibi was silent, very pale. All the prisoners in the block stood naked between the beds. This must be how one stands at the last judgment.

"They're coming!"

There were three SS officers standing round the notorious Dr. Mengele, who had received us at Birkenau. The head of the block, with an attempt at a smile, asked us:

"Ready?"

Yes, we were ready. So were the SS doctors. Dr. Mengele was holding a list in his hand: our numbers. He made a sign to the head of the block: "We can begin!" As if this were a game!

The first to go by were the "officials" of the block: *Stubenaelteste*, Kapos, foremen, all in perfect physical condition of course! Then came the ordinary prisoners' turn. Dr. Mengele took stock of them from head to foot. Every now and then, he wrote a number down. One single thought filled my mind: not to let my number be taken; not to show my left arm.

There were only Tibi and Yossi in front of me. They passed. I had time to notice that Mengele had not written their numbers down. Someone pushed me. It was my turn.

I ran without looking back. My head was spinning: you're too thin, you're weak, you're too thin, you're good for the furnace. . . . The race seemed interminable. I thought I had been running for years. . . . You're too thin, you're too weak. . . . At last I had arrived exhausted. When I regained my breath, I questioned Yossi and Tibi:

"Was I written down?"

"No," said Yossi. He added, smiling: "In any case, he couldn't have written you down, you were running too fast. . . ."

I began to laugh. I was glad. I would have liked to kiss him. At that moment, what did the others matter! I hadn't been written down.

Those whose numbers had been noted stood apart, abandoned by the whole world. Some were weeping in silence.

The SS officers went away. The head of the block appeared, his face reflecting the general weariness.

"Everything went off all right. Don't worry. Nothing is going to happen to anyone. To anyone."

Again he tried to smile. A poor, emaciated, dried-up Jew questioned him avidly in a trembling voice:

"But . . . but, *Blockaelteste*, they did write me down!"

The head of the block let his anger break out. What! Did someone refuse to believe him!

"What's the matter now? Am I telling lies then? I tell you once and for all, nothing's going to happen to you! To anyone! You're wallowing in your own despair, you fool!"

The bell rang, a signal that the selection had been completed throughout the camp.

With all my might I began to run to Block 36. I met my father on the way. He came up to me:

"Well? So you passed?"

"Yes. And you?"

"Me too."

How we breathed again, now! My father had brought

me a present—half a ration of bread obtained in exchange for a piece of rubber, found at the warehouse, which would do to sole a shoe.

The bell. Already we must separate, go to bed. Everything was regulated by the bell. It gave me orders, and I automatically obeyed them. I hated it. Whenever I dreamed of a better world, I could only imagine a universe with no bells.

Several days had elapsed. We no longer thought about the selection. We went to work as usual, loading heavy stones into railway wagons. Rations had become more meager: this was the only change.

We had risen before dawn, as on every day. We had received the black coffee, the ration of bread. We were about to set out for the yard as usual. The head of the block arrived, running.

"Silence for a moment. I have a list of numbers here. I'm going to read them to you. Those whose numbers I call won't be going to work this morning; they'll stay behind in the camp."

And, in a soft voice, he read out about ten numbers. We had understood. These were numbers chosen at the selection. Dr. Mengele had not forgotten.

The head of the block went toward his room. Ten prisoners surrounded him, hanging onto his clothes:

"Save us! You promised . . .! We want to go to the yard. We're strong enough to work. We're good workers. We can . . . we will . . . ."

He tried to calm them, to reassure them about their fate, to explain to them that the fact that they were staying behind in the camp did not mean much, had no tragic significance.

"After all, I stay here myself every day," he added.

It was a somewhat feeble argument. He realized it, and without another word went and shut himself up in his room.

The bell had just rung.

"Form up!"

It scarcely mattered now that the work was hard. The essential thing was to be as far away as possible from the block, from the crucible of death, from the center of hell.

I saw my father running toward me. I became frightened all of a sudden.

"What's the matter?"

Out of breath, he could hardly open his mouth.

"Me, too . . . me, too . . .! They told me to stay behind in the camp."

They had written down his number without his being aware of it.

"What will happen?" I asked in anguish.

But it was he who tried to reassure me.

"It isn't certain yet. There's still a chance of escape. They're going to do another selection today . . . a decisive selection."

I was silent.

He felt that his time was short. He spoke quickly. He would have liked to say so many things. His speech grew confused; his voice choked. He knew that I would have to go in a few moments. He would have to stay behind alone, so very alone.

"Look, take this knife," he said to me. "I don't need it any longer. It might be useful to you. And take this spoon as well. Don't sell them. Quickly! Go on. Take what I'm giving you!"

The inheritance.

"Don't talk like that, father." (I felt that I would break into sobs.) "I don't want you to say that. Keep the spoon and knife. You need them as much as I do. We shall see each other again this evening, after work."

He looked at me with his tired eyes, veiled with despair. He went on:

"I'm asking this of you. . . . Take them. Do as I ask, my son. We have no time. . . . Do as your father asks."

Our Kapo yelled that we should start.

The unit set out toward the camp gate. Left, right! I bit my lips. My father had stayed by the block, leaning against the wall. Then he began to run, to catch up with us. Perhaps he had forgotten something he wanted to say to me. . . . But we were marching too quicly. . . . Left, right!

We were already at the gate. They counted us, to the din of military music. We were outside.

The whole day, I wandered about as if sleepwalking. Now and then Tibi and Yossi would throw me a brotherly word. The Kapo, too, tried to reassure me. He had given me easier work today. I felt sick at heart. How well they were treating me! Like an orphan! I thought: even now, my father is still helping me.

I did not know myself what I wanted—for the day to pass quickly or not. I was afraid of finding myself alone that night. How good it would be to die here!

At last we began the return journey. How I longed for orders to run!

The military march. The gate. The camp.

I ran to Block 36.

Were there still miracles on this earth? He was alive. He had escaped the second selection. He had been able to prove that he was still useful. . . . I gave him back his knife and spoon.

Akiba Drumer left us, a victim of the selection. Lately, he had wandered among us, his eyes glazed, telling everyone of his weakness: "I can't go on . . . It's all over. . . ." It was impossible to raise his morale. He didn't listen to what we told him. He could only repeat that all was over for him, that he could no longer keep up the struggle, that he had no strength left, nor faith. Suddenly his eyes would become blank, nothing but two open wounds, two pits of terror.

He was not the only one to lose his faith during those selection days. I knew a rabbi from a little town in Poland, a bent old man, whose lips were always trembling. He used to pray all the time, in the block, in the yard, in the ranks. He would recite whole pages of the Talmud from memory, argue with himself, ask himself questions and answer himself. And one day he said to me: "It's the end. God is no longer with us."

And, as though he had repented of having spoken such words, so clipped, so cold, he added in his faint voice:

"I know. One has no right to say things like that. I know. Man is too small, too humble and inconsiderable to seek to understand the mysterious ways of God. But what can I do? I'm not a sage, one of the elect, nor a saint. I'm just an ordinary creature of flesh and blood. I've got eyes, too, and I can see what they're doing here. Where is the divine Mercy? Where is God? How can I believe, how could anyone believe, in this merciful God?"

Poor Akiba Drumer, if he could have gone on believing in God, if he could have seen a proof of God in this Calvary, he would not have been taken by the selection. But as soon as he felt the first cracks forming in his faith, he had lost his reason for struggling and had begun to die.

When the selection came, he was condemned in advance, offering his own neck to the executioner. All he asked of us was:

"In three days I shall no longer be here. . . . Say the Kaddish for me."

We promised him. In three days' time, when we saw the smoke rising from the chimney, we would think of him. Ten of us would gather together and hold a special service. All his friends would say the Kaddish.

Then he went off toward the hospital, his step steadier, not looking back. An ambulance was waiting to take him to Birkenau.

These were terrible days. We received more blows than food; we were crushed with work. And three days after he had gone we forgot to say the Kaddish.

Winter had come. The days were short, and the nights

had become almost unbearable. In the first hours of dawn, the icy wind cut us like a whip. We were given winter clothes—slightly thicker striped shirts. The veterans found in this a new source of derision.

"Now you'll really be getting a taste of the camp!"

We left for work as usual, our bodies frozen. The stones were so cold that it seemed as though our hands would be glued to them if we touched them. But you get used to anything.

On Christmas and New Year's Day, there was no work.

We were allowed a slightly thicker soup.

Toward the middle of January, my right foot began to swell because of the cold. I was unable to put it on the ground. I went to have it examined. The doctor, a great Jewish doctor, a prisoner like ourselves, was quite definite: I must have an operation! If we waited, the toes—and perhaps the whole leg—would have to be amputated.

This was the last straw! But I had no choice. The doctor had decided on an operation, and there was no discussing it. I was even glad that it was he who had made the decision.

They put me into a bed with white sheets. I had forgotten that people slept in sheets.

The hospital was not bad at all. We were given good bread and thicker soup. No more bell. No more roll call. No more work. Now and then I was able to send a bit of bread to my father.

Near me lay a Hungarian Jew who had been struck down with dysentery—skin and bone, with dead eyes. I could only hear his voice; it was the sole indication that he was alive. Where did he get the strength to talk?

"You mustn't rejoice too soon, my boy. There's selection here too. More often than outside. Germany doesn't need sick Jews. Germany doesn't need me. When the next transport comes, you'll have a new neighbor. So listen to me, and take my advice: get out of the hospital before the next selection!"

These words which came from under the ground, from

a faceless shape, filled me with terror. It was indeed true that the hospital was very small and that if new invalids arrived in the next few days, room would have to be found for them.

But perhaps my faceless neighbor, fearing that he would be among the first victims, simply wanted to drive me away, to free my bed in order to give himself a chance to survive. Perhaps he just wanted to frighten me. Yet, what if he were telling the truth? I decided to await events.

The doctor came to tell me that the operation would be the next day.

"Don't be afraid," he added. "Everything will be all right."

At ten o'clock in the morning, they took me into the operating room. "My" doctor was there. I took comfort from this. I felt that nothing serious could happen while he was there. There was balm in every word he spoke, and every glance he gave me held a message of hope.

"It will hurt you a bit," he said, "but that will pass. Grit your teeth."

The operation lasted an hour. They had not put me to sleep. I kept my eyes fixed upon my doctor. Then I felt myself go under. . . .

When I came round, opening my eyes, I could see nothing at first but a great whiteness, my sheets; then I noticed the face of my doctor, bending over me:

"Everything went off well. You're brave, my boy. Now you're going to stay here for two weeks, rest comfortably, and it will be over. You'll eat well, and relax your body and your nerves."

I could only follow the movements of his lips. I scarcely understood what he was saying, but the murmur of his voice did me good. Suddenly a cold sweat broke out on my forehead. I could not feel my leg! Had they amputated it?

"Doctor," I stammered. "Doctor . . . ?"

"What's the matter, son?"

I lacked the courage to ask him the question.

"Doctor, I'm thirsty . . . ."

He had water brought to me. He was smiling. He was getting ready to go and visit the other patients.

"Doctor?"

"What?"

"Shall I still be able to use my leg?"

He was no longer smiling. I was very frightened. He said:

"Do you trust me, my boy?"

"I trust you absolutely, Doctor."

"Well then, listen to me. You'll be completely recovered in a fortnight. You'll be able to walk like anyone else. The sole of your foot was all full of pus. We just had to open the swelling. You haven't had your leg amputated. You'll see. In a fortnight's time you'll be walking about like everyone else."

I had only a fortnight to wait.

Two days after my operation, there was a rumor going round the camp that the front had suddenly drawn nearer. The Red Army, they said, was advancing on Buna; it was only a matter of hours now.

We were already accustomed to rumors of this kind. It was not the first time a false prophet had foretold to us peace-on-earth, negotiations-with-the-Red-Cross-for-our-release, or other false rumors. . . . And often we believed them. It was an injection of morphine.

But this time these prophecies seemed more solid. During these last few nights, we had heard the guns in the distance.

My neighbor, the faceless one, said:

"Don't let yourself be fooled with illusions. Hitler has made it very clear that he will annihilate all the Jews before the clock strikes twelve, before they can hear the last stroke."

I burst out:

"What does it matter to you? Do we have to regard Hitler as a prophet?"

His glazed, faded eyes looked at me. At last he said in a weary voice:

"I've got more faith in Hitler than in anyone else. He's the only one who's kept his promises, all his promises, to the Jewish people."

At four o'clock on the afternoon of the same day, as usual the bell summoned all the heads of the blocks to go and report.

They came back shattered. They could only just open their lips enough to say the word: evacuation. The camp was to be emptied, and we were to be sent farther back. Where to? To somewhere right in the depths of Germany, to other camps; there was no shortage of them.

"When?"

"Tomorrow evening."

"Perhaps the Russians will arrive first."

"Perhaps."

We knew perfectly well that they would not.

The camp had become a hive. People ran about, shouting at one another. In all the blocks, preparations for the journey were going on. I had forgotten about my bad foot. A doctor came into the room and announced:

"Tomorrow, immediately after nightfall, the camp will set out. Block after block. Patients will stay in the infirmary. They will not be evacuated."

This news made us think. Were the SS going to leave hundreds of prisoners to strut about in the hospital blocks, waiting for their liberators? Were they going to let the Jews hear the twelfth stroke sound? Obviously not.

"All the invalids will be summarily killed," said the faceless one. "And sent to the crematory in a final batch."

"The camp is certain to be mined," said another. "The moment the evacuation's over, it'll blow up."

As for me, I was not thinking about death, but I did not want to be separated from my father. We had already suffered so much, borne so much together; this was not the time to be separated.

I ran outside to look for him. The snow was thick, and the windows of the blocks were veiled with frost. One shoe in my hand, because it would not go onto my right foot, I ran on, feeling neither pain nor cold.

"What shall we do?"

My father did not answer.

"What shall we do, father?"

He was lost in thought. The choice was in our hands. For once we could decide our fate for ourselves. We could both stay in the hospital, where I could, thanks to my doctor, get him entered as a patient or a nurse. Or else we could follow the others.

"Well, what shall we do, father?"

He was silent.

"Let's be evacuated with the others," I said to him.

He did not answer. He looked at my foot.

"Do you think you can walk?"

"Yes, I think so."

"Let's hope that we shan't regret it, Eliezer."

I learned after the war the fate of those who had stayed behind in the hospital. They were quite simply liberated by the Russians two days after the evacuation.

I did not go back to the hospital again. I returned to my block. My wound was open and bleeding; the snow had grown red where I had trodden.

The head of the block gave out double rations of bread and margarine, for the journey. We could take as many shirts and other clothes as we liked from the store.

It was cold. We got into bed.

The last night in Buna. Yet another last night. The last night at home, the last night in the ghetto, the last night in the train, and, now, the last night in Buna. How much longer were our lives to be dragged out from one "last night" to another?

I did not sleep at all. Through the frosted panes bursts of red light could be seen. Cannon shots split the night-time silence. How close the Russians were! Between them and us—one night, our last night. There was whispering from one bed to another: with luck the Russians would be here before the evacuation. Hope revived again.

Someone shouted:

"Try and sleep. Gather your strength for the journey."

This reminded me of my mother's last words of advice in the ghetto.

But I could not sleep. My foot felt as if it were burning.

In the morning, the face of the camp had changed. Prisoners appeared in strange outfits: it was like a masquerade. Everyone had put on several garments, one on top of the other, in order to keep out the cold. Poor mountebanks, wider than they were tall, more dead than alive; poor clowns, their ghostlike faces emerging from piles of prison clothes! Buffoons!

I tried to find a shoe that was too large. In vain. I tore up a blanket and wrapped my wounded foot in it. Then I went wandering through the camp, looking for a little more bread and a few potatoes.

Some said we were being taken to Czechoslovakia. No, to Gros-Rosen. No, to Gleiwitz. No, to. . . .

Two o'clock in the afternoon. The snow was still coming down thickly.

The time was passing quickly now. Dusk had fallen. The day was disappearing in a monochrome of gray.

The head of the block suddenly remembered that he had forgotten to clean out the block. He ordered four prisoners to wash the wooden floor. . . . An hour before leaving the camp! Why? For whom?

"For the liberating army," he cried. "So that they'll realize there were men living here and not pigs."

Were we men then? The block was cleaned from top to bottom, washed in every corner.

At six o'clock the bell rang. The death knell. The burial. The procession was about to begin its march.

"Form up! Quickly!"

In a few moments we were all in rows, by blocks. Night had fallen. Everything was in order, according to the prearranged plan.

The searchlights came on. Hundreds of armed SS men rose up out of the darkness, accompanied by sheepdogs. The snow never ceased.

The gates of the camp opened. It seemed that an even darker night was waiting for us on the other side.

The first blocks began to march. We waited. We had to wait for the departure of the fifty-six blocks who came before us. It was very cold. In my pocket I had two pieces of bread. With how much pleasure could I have eaten them! But I was not allowed to. Not yet.

Our turn was coming: Block 53 . . . Block 55 . . .

Block 57, forward march!

It snowed relentlessly.

An icy wind blew in violent gusts. But we marched without faltering.

The SS made us increase our pace. "Faster, you swine, you filthy sons of bitches!" Why not? The movement warmed us up a little. The blood flowed more easily in our veins. One felt oneself reviving. . . .

"Faster, you filthy sons of bitches!" We were no longer marching; we were running. Like automatons. The SS were running too, their weapons in their hands. We looked as though we were fleeing before them.

Pitch darkness. Every now and then, an explosion in the night. They had orders to fire on any who could not keep up. Their fingers on the triggers, they did not deprive themselves of this pleasure. If one of us stopped for a second, a sharp shot finished off another filthy son of a bitch.

I was putting one foot in front of the other mechanically. I was dragging with me this skeletal body which weighed so much. If only I could have got rid of it! In spite of my efforts not to think about it, I could feel myself as two entities—my body and me. I hated it.

I repeated to myself: "Don't think. Don't stop. Run."

Near me, men were collapsing in the dirty snow. Shots.

At my side marched a young Polish lad called Zalman. He had been working in the electrical warehouse at Buna. They had laughed at him because he was always praying or meditating on some problem of the Talmud. It was his way of escaping from reality, of not feeling the blows. . . .

He was suddenly seized with cramp in the stomach. "I've got stomach ache," he whispered to me. He could not go on. He had to stop for a moment. I begged him:

"Wait a bit, Zalman. We shall all be stopping soon. We're not going to run like this till the end of the world."

But as he ran he began to undo his buttons, crying:

"I can't go on any longer. My stomach's bursting. . . ."

"Make an effort, Zalman. . . . Try. . . ."

"I can't. . . ." he groaned.

His trousers lowered, he let himself sink down.

That is the last picture I have of him. I do not think it can have been the SS who finished him, because no one had noticed. He must have been trampled to death beneath the feet of the thousands of men who followed us.

I quickly forgot him. I began to think of myself again. Because of my painful foot, a shudder went through me at each step. "A few more yards," I thought. "A few more yards, and that will be the end. I shall fall. A spurt of red flame. A shot." Death wrapped itself around me till I was stifled. It stuck to me. I felt that I could touch it. The idea of dying, of no longer being, began to fascinate me. Not to exist any longer. Not to feel the horrible pains in my foot. Not to feel anything, neither weariness, nor cold, nor anything. To break the ranks, to let oneself slide to the edge of the road. . . .

My father's presence was the only thing that stopped me. . . . He was running at my side, out of breath, at the end of his strength, at his wit's end. I had no right to let myself die. What would he do without me? I was his only support.

These thoughts had taken up a brief space of time, during which I had gone on running without feeling my throbbing foot, without realizing that I was running, without being conscious that I owned a body galloping there on the road in the midst of so many thousands of others.

When I came to myself again, I tried to slacken the pace. But there was no way. A great tidal wave of men came rolling onward and would have crushed me like an ant.

I was simply walking in my sleep. I managed to close my eyes and to run like that while asleep. Now and then, someone would push me violently from behind, and I would wake up. The other would shout: "Run faster. If you don't want to go on, let other people come past." All I had to do was to close my eyes for a second to see a whole world passing by, to dream a whole lifetime.

An endless road. Letting oneself be pushed by the mob; letting oneself be dragged along by a blind destiny. When the SS became tired, they were changed. But no one changed us. Our limbs numb with cold despite the running, our throats parched, famished, breathless, on we went.

We were masters of nature, masters of the world. We had forgotten everything—death, fatigue, our natural needs. Stronger than cold or hunger, stronger than the shots and the desire to die, condemned and wandering, mere numbers, we were the only men on earth.

At last, the morning star appeared in the gray sky. A trail of indeterminate light showed on the horizon. We were exhausted. We were without strength, without illusions.

The commandant announced that we had already covered forty-two miles since we left. It was a long time since we had passed beyond the limits of fatigue. Our legs were moving mechanically, in spite of us, without us.

We went through a deserted village. Not a living soul.

Not the bark of a dog. Houses with gaping windows. A few slipped out of the ranks to try and hide in some deserted building.

Still one hour's marching more, and at last came the order to rest.

We sank down as one man in the snow. My father shook me.

"Not here. . . . Get up. . . . A little farther on. There's a shed over there . . . come on."

I had neither the will nor the strength to get up. Nevertheless I obeyed. It was not a shed, but a brick factory with a caved-in roof, broken windows, walls filthy with soot. It was not easy to get in. Hundreds of prisoners were crowding at the door.

We at last succeeded in getting inside. There too the snow was thick. I let myself sink down. It was only then that I really felt my weariness. The snow was like a carpet, very gentle, very warm. I fell asleep.

I do not know how long I slept. A few moments or an hour. When I woke up, a frozen hand was patting my cheeks. I forced myself to open my eyes. It was my father.

How old he had grown since the night before! His body was completely twisted, shriveled up into itself. His eyes were petrified, his lips withered, decayed. Everything about him bore witness to extreme exhaustion. His voice was damp with tears and snow:

"Don't let yourself be overcome by sleep, Eliezer. It's dangerous to fall asleep in the snow. You might sleep for good. Come on, come on. Get up."

Get up? How could I? How could I get myself out of this fluffy bed? I could hear what my father said, but it seemed empty of meaning, as though he had told me to lift up the whole building in my arms. . . .

"Come on, son, come on. . . ."

I got up, gritting my teeth. Supporting me with his arm, he led me outside. It was far from easy. It was as difficult to go out as to get in. Under our feet were men crushed, trampled underfoot, dying. No one paid any attention.

We were outside. The icy wind stung my face. I bit my lips continually to prevent them from freezing. Around me everything was dancing a dance of death. It made my head reel. I was walking in a cemetery, among stiffened corpses, logs of wood. Not a cry of distress, not a groan, nothing but a mass agony, in silence. No one asked anyone else for help. You died because you had to die. There was no fuss.

In every stiffened corpse I saw myself. And soon I should not even see them; I should be one of them—a matter of hours.

"Come on, father, let's go back to the shed. . . ."

He did not answer. He was not looking at the dead.

"Come on, father, it's better over there. We can lie down a bit, one after the other. I'll watch over you, and then you can watch over me. We won't let each other fall asleep. We'll look after each other."

He agreed. Trampling over living bodies and corpses, we managed to re-enter the shed. Here we let ourselves sink down.

"Don't be afraid, son. Sleep—you can sleep. I'll look after you myself."

"No, you first, father. Go to sleep."

He refused. I lay down and tried to force myself to sleep, to doze a little, but in vain. God knows what I would not have given for a few moments of sleep. But, deep down, I felt that to sleep would mean to die. And something within me revolted against this death. All round me death was moving in, silently, without violence. It would seize upon some sleeping being, enter into him, and consume him bit by bit. Next to me there was someone trying to wake up his neighbor, his brother, perhaps, or a friend. In vain. Discouraged in the attempt, the man lay down in his turn, next to the corpse, and slept too. Who was there to wake him up? Stretching out an arm, I touched him:

"Wake up. You mustn't sleep here. . . ."

He half opened his eyes.

"No advice," he said in a faint voice. "I'm tired. Leave me alone. Leave me."

My father, too, was gently dozing. I could not see his eyes. His cap had fallen over his face.

"Wake up," I whispered in his ear.

He started up. He sat up and looked round him, bewildered, stupefied—a bereaved stare. He stared all round him in a circle as though he had suddenly decided to draw up an inventory of his universe, to find out exactly where he was, in what place, and why. Then he smiled.

I shall always remember that smile. From which world did it come?

The snow continued to fall in thick flakes over the corpses.

The door of the shed opened. An old man appeared, his moustache covered with frost, his lips blue with cold. It was Rabbi Eliahou, the rabbi of a small Polish community. He was a very good man, well loved by everyone in the camp, even by the Kapos and the heads of the blocks. Despite the trials and privations, his face still shone with his inner purity. He was the only rabbi who was always addressed as "Rabbi" at Buna. He was like one of the old prophets, always in the midst of his people to comfort them. And, strangely, his words of comfort never provoked rebellion; they really brought peace.

He came into the shed and his eyes, brighter than ever, seemed to be looking for someone:

"Perhaps someone has seen my son somewhere?"

He had lost his son in the crowd. He had looked in vain among the dying. Then he had scratched up the snow to find his corpse. Without result.

For three years they had stuck together. Always near each other, for suffering, for blows, for the ration of bread, for prayer. Three years, from camp to camp, from selection to selection. And now—when the end seemed near—fate had separated them. Finding himself near me, Rabbi Eliahou whispered:

"It happened on the road. We lost sight of one another during the journey. I had stayed a little to the rear of the column. I hadn't any strength left for running. And my son didn't notice. That's all I know. Where has he disappeared? Where can I find him? Perhaps you've seen him somewhere?"

"No, Rabbi Eliahou, I haven't seen him."

He left then as he had come: like a wind-swept shadow.

He had already passed through the door when I suddenly remembered seeing his son running by my side. I had forgotten that, and I didn't tell Rabbi Eliahou!

Then I remembered something else: his son had seen him losing ground, limping, staggering back to the rear of the column. He had seen him. And he had continued to run on in front, letting the distance between them grow greater.

A terrible thought loomed up in my mind: he had wanted to get rid of his father! He had felt that his father was growing weak, he had believed that the end was near and had sought this separation in order to get rid of the burden, to free himself from an encumbrance which could lessen his own chances of survival.

I had done well to forget that. And I was glad that Rabbi Eliahou should continue to look for his beloved son.

And, in spite of myself, a prayer rose in my heart, to that God in whom I no longer believed.

My God, Lord of the Universe, give me strength never to do what Rabbi Eliahou's son has done.

Shouts rose outside in the yard, where darkness had fallen. The SS ordered the ranks to form up.

The march began again. The dead stayed in the yard under the snow, like faithful guards assassinated, without burial. No one had said the prayer for the dead over them. Sons abandoned their fathers' remains without a tear.

On the way it snowed, snowed, snowed endlessly. We

were marching more slowly. The guards themselves seemed tired. My wounded foot no longer hurt me. It must have been completely frozen. The foot was lost to me. It had detached itself from my body like the wheel of a car. Too bad. I should have to resign myself; I could live with only one leg. The main thing was not to think about it. Above all, not at this moment. Leave thoughts for later.

Our march had lost all semblance of discipline. We went as we wanted, as we could. We heard no more shots. Our guards must have been tired.

But death scarcely needed any help from them. The cold was conscientiously doing its work. At every step some-one fell and suffered no more.

From time to time, SS officers on motorcycles would go down the length of the column to try and shake us out of our growing apathy:

"Keep going! We are getting there!"

"Courage! Only a few more hours!"

"We're reaching Gleiwitz."

These words of encouragement, even though they came from the mouths of our assassins, did us a great deal of good. No one wanted to give up now, just before the end, so near to the goal. Our eyes searched the horizon for the barbed wire of Gleiwitz. Our only desire was to reach it as quickly as possible.

The night had now set in. The snow had ceased to fall. We walked for several more hours before arriving.

We did not notice the camp until we were just in front of the gate.

Some Kapos rapidly installed us in the barracks. We pushed and jostled one another as if this were the supreme refuge, the gateway to life. We walked over pain-racked bodies. We trod on wounded faces. No cries. A few groans. My father and I were ourselves thrown to the ground by this rolling tide. Beneath our feet someone let out a rattling cry:

"You're crushing me . . . mercy!"

A voice that was not unknown to me.

"You're crushing me . . . mercy! mercy!"

The same faint voice, the same rattle, heard somewhere before. That voice had spoken to me one day. Where? When? Years ago? No, it could only have been at the camp.

"Mercy!"

I felt that I was crushing him. I was stopping his breath. I wanted to get up. I struggled to disengage myself, so that he could breathe. But I was crushed myself beneath the weight of other bodies. I could hardly breathe. I dug my nails into unknown faces. I was biting all round me, in order to get air. No one cried out.

Suddenly I remembered. Juliek! The boy from Warsaw who played the violin in the band at Buna. . . .

"Juliek, is it you?"

"Eliezer . . . the twenty-five strokes of the whip. Yes . . . I remember."

He was silent. A long moment elapsed.

"Juliek! Can you hear me, Juliek?"

"Yes . . . ," he said, in a feeble voice. "What do you want?"

He was not dead.

"How do you feel, Juliek?" I asked, less to know the answer than to hear that he could speak, that he was alive.

"All right, Eliezer. . . . I'm getting on all right . . . hardly any air . . . worn out. My feet are swollen. It's good to rest, but my violin. . . ."

I thought he had gone out of his mind. What use was the violin here?

"What, your violin?"

He gasped.

"I'm afraid . . . I'm afraid . . . that they'll break my violin. . . . I've brought it with me."

I could not answer him. Someone was lying full length on top of me, covering my face. I was unable to breathe, through either mouth or nose. Sweat beaded my brow, ran down my spine. This was the end—the end of the road. A silent death, suffocation. No way of crying out, of calling for help.

I tried to get rid of my invisible assassin. My whole will to live was centered in my nails. I scratched. I battled for a mouthful of air. I tore at decaying flesh which did not respond. I could not free myself from this mass weighing down my chest. Was it a dead man I was struggling against? Who knows?

I shall never know. All I can say is that I won. I succeeded in digging a hole through this wall of dying people, a little hole through which I could drink in a small quantity of air.

"Father, how are you?" I asked, as soon as I could utter a word.

I knew he could not be far from me.

"Well!" answered a distant voice, which seemed to come from another world. I tried to sleep.

He tried to sleep. Was he right or wrong? Could one sleep here? Was it not dangerous to allow your vigilance to fail, even for a moment, when at any minute death could pounce upon you?

I was thinking of this when I heard the sound of a violin. The sound of a violin, in this dark shed, where the dead were heaped on the living. What madman could be playing the violin here, at the brink of his own grave? Or was it really an hallucination?

It must have been Juliek.

He played a fragment from Beethoven's concerto. I had never heard sounds so pure. In such a silence.

How had he managed to free himself? To draw his body from under mine without my being aware of it?

It was pitch dark. I could hear only the violin, and it was as though Juliek's soul were the bow. He was playing his life. The whole of his life was gliding on the strings—his lost hopes, his charred past, his extinguished future. He played as he would never play again.

I shall never forget Juliek. How could I forget that concert, given to an audience of dying and dead men! To this day, whenever I hear Beethoven played my eyes close and out of the dark rises the sad, pale face of my Polish friend, as he said farewell on his violin to an audience of dying men.

I do not know for how long he played. I was overcome by sleep. When I awoke, in the daylight, I could see Juliek, opposite me, slumped over, dead. Near him lay his violin, smashed, trampled, a strange overwhelming little corpse.

We stayed at Gleiwitz for three days. Three days without food or drink. We were not allowed to leave the barracks. SS men guarded the door.

I was hungry and thirsty. I must have been very dirty and exhausted, to judge from the appearance of the others. The bread we had brought from Buna had long since been devoured. And who knew when we would be given another ration?

The front was following us. We could hear new gun shots again, very close. But we had neither the strength nor the courage to believe that the Nazis would not have time to evacuate us, and that the Russians would soon be here.

We heard that we were going to be deported into the center of Germany.

On the third day, at dawn, we were driven out of the barracks. We all threw blankets over our shoulders, like prayer shawls. We were directed toward a gate which divided the camp into two. A group of SS officers were standing there. A rumor ran through our ranks—a selection!

The SS officers did the selecting. The weak, to the left; those who could walk well, to the right.

My father was sent to the left. I ran after him. An SS officer shouted at my back:

"Come back here!"

I slipped in among the others. Several SS rushed to bring me back, creating such confusion that many of the people from the left were able to come back to the right—and among them, my father and myself. However, there were some shots and some dead.

We were all made to leave the camp. After half an hour's marching we arrived right in the middle of a field divided by rails. We had to wait for the train to arrive.

The snow fell thickly. We were forbidden to sit down or even to move.

The snow began to form a thick layer over our blankets. They brought us bread—the usual ration. We threw ourselves upon it. Someone had the idea of appeasing his thirst by eating the snow. Soon the others were imitating him. As we were not allowed to bend down, everyone took out his spoon and ate the accumulated snow off his neighbor's back. A mouthful of bread and a spoonful of snow. The SS who were watching laughed at this spectacle.

Hours went by. Our eyes grew weary of scouring the horizon for the liberating train. It did not arrive until much later in the evening. An infinitely long train, composed of cattle wagons, with no roofs. The SS pushed us in, a hundred to a carriage, we were so thin! Our embarkation completed, the convoy set out.

Pressed up against the others in an effort to keep out the cold, head empty and heavy at the same time, brain a whirlpool of decaying memories. Indifference deadened the spirit. Here or elsewhere—what difference did it make? To die today or tomorrow, or later? The night was long and never ending.

When at last a gray glimmer of light appeared on the horizon, it revealed a tangle of human shapes, heads sunk upon shoulders, crouched, piled one on top of the other, like a field of dust-covered tombstones in the first light of the dawn. I tried to distinguish those who were still alive from those who had gone. But there was no difference. My gaze was held for a long time by one who lay with his eyes open, staring into the void. His livid face was covered with a layer of frost and snow.

My father was huddled near me, wrapped in his blanket, his shoulders covered with snow. And was he dead, too? I called him. No answer. I would have cried out if I could have done so. He did not move.

My mind was invaded suddenly by this realization—there was no more reason to live, no more reason to struggle.

The train stopped in the middle of a deserted field. The suddenness of the halt woke some of those who were asleep. They straightened themselves up, throwing startled looks around them.

Outside, the SS went by, shouting:

"Throw out all the dead! All corpses outside!"

The living rejoiced. There would be more room. Volunteers set to work. They felt those who were still crouching.

"Here's one! Take him!"

They undressed him, the survivors avidly sharing out his clothes, then two "gravediggers" took him, one by the head and one by the feet, and threw him out of the wagon like a sack of flour.

From all directions came cries:

"Come on! Here's one! This man next to me. He doesn't move."

I woke from my apathy just at the moment when two men came up to my father. I threw myself on top of his body. He was cold. I slapped him. I rubbed his hands, crying:

"Father! Father! Wake up. They're trying to throw you out of the carriage. . . ."

His body remained inert.

The two gravediggers seized me by the collar.

"Leave him. You can see perfectly well that he's dead."

"No!" I cried. "He isn't dead! Not yet!"

I set to work to slap him as hard as I could. After a moment my father's eyelids moved slightly over his glazed eyes. He was breathing weakly.

"You see," I cried.

The two men moved away.

Twenty bodies were thrown out of our wagon. Then the train resumed its journey, leaving behind it a few hundred naked dead, deprived of burial, in the deep snow of a field in Poland.

We were given no food. We lived on snow; it took the place of bread. The days were like nights, and the nights left the dregs of their darkness in our souls. The train was traveling slowly, often stopping for several hours and then setting off again. It never ceased snowing. All through these days and nights we stayed crouching, one on top of the other, never speaking a word. We were no more than frozen bodies. Our eyes closed, we waited merely for the next stop, so that we could unload our dead.

Ten days, ten nights of traveling. Sometimes we would pass through German townships. Very early in the morning, usually. The workmen were going to work. They stopped and stared after us, but otherwise showed no surprise.

One day when we had stopped, a workman took a piece of bread out of his bag and threw it into a wagon. There was a stampede. Dozens of starving men fought each other to the death for a few crumbs. The German workmen took a lively interest in this spectacle.

Some years later, I watched the same kind of scene at Aden. The passengers on our boat were amusing themselves by throwing coins to the "natives," who were diving in to get them. An attractive, aristocratic Parisienne was deriving special pleasure from the game. I suddenly noticed that two children were engaged in a death struggle, trying to strangle each other. I turned to the lady.

"Please," I begged, "don't throw any more money in!"

"Why not?" she said. "I like to give charity. . . ."

In the wagon where the bread had fallen, a real battle had broken out. Men threw themselves on top of each other, stamping on each other, tearing at each other, biting each other. Wild beasts of prey, with animal hatred in their eyes; an extraordinary vitality had seized them, sharpening their teeth and nails.

A crowd of workmen and curious spectators had collected along the train. They had probably never seen a train with such a cargo. Soon, nearly everywhere, pieces of bread were being dropped into the wagons. The audience stared at these skeletons of men, fighting one another to the death for a mouthful.

A piece fell into our wagon. I decided that I would not move. Anyway, I knew that I would never have the strength to fight with a dozen savage men! Not far away I noticed an old man dragging himself along on all fours. He was trying to disengage himself from the struggle. He held one hand to his heart. I thought at first he had received a blow in the chest. Then I understood; he had a bit of bread under his shirt. With remarkable speed he drew it out and put it to his mouth. His eyes gleamed; a smile, like a grimace, lit up his dead face. And was immediately extinguished. A shadow had just loomed up near him. The shadow threw itself upon him. Felled to the ground, stunned with blows, the old man cried:

"Meir. Meir, my boy! Don't you recognize me? I'm your father . . . you're hurting me . . . you're killing your father! I've got some bread . . . for you too . . . for you too. . . ."

He collapsed. His fist was still clenched around a small piece. He tried to carry it to his mouth. But the other one threw himself upon him and snatched it. The old man again whispered something, let out a rattle, and died amid the general indifference. His son searched him, took the bread, and began to devour it. He was not able to get very far. Two men had seen and hurled themselves upon him. Others joined in. When they withdrew, next to me were two corpses, side by side, the father and the son.

I was fifteen years old.

In our wagon, there was a friend of my father's called Meir Katz. He had worked as a gardener at Buna and used to bring us a few green vegetables occasionally. Being less undernourished than the rest of us, he had stood up to imprisonment better. Because he was relatively more vigorous, he had been put in charge of the wagon.

On the third night of our journey I woke up suddenly and felt two hands on my throat, trying to strangle me. I just had the time to shout, "Father!"

Nothing but this word. I felt myself suffocating. But my father had woken up and seized my attacker. Too weak to overcome him, he had the idea of calling Meir Katz.

"Come here! Come quickly! There's someone strangling my son."

A few moments later I was free. I still do not know why the man wanted to strangle me.

After a few days, Meir Katz spoke to my father:

"Chlomo, I'm getting weak. I'm losing my strength. I can't hold on. . . ."

"Don't let yourself go under," my father said, trying to encourage him. "You must resist. Don't lose faith in yourself."

But Meir Katz groaned heavily in reply.

"I can't go on any longer, Chlomo! What can I do? I can't carry on. . . ."

My father took his arm. And Meir Katz, the strong man, the most robust of us all, wept. His son had been taken from him at the time of the first selection, but it was now that he wept. It was now that he cracked up. He was finished, at the end of his tether.

On the last day of our journey a terrible wind arose; it snowed without ceasing. We felt that the end was near—the real end. We could never hold out in this icy wind, in these gusts.

Someone got up and shouted:

"We mustn't stay sitting down at a time like this. We shall freeze to death! Let's all get up and move a bit. . . ."

We all got up. We held our damp blankets more tightly around us. And we forced ourselves to move a few steps, to turn around where we were.

Suddenly a cry rose up from the wagon, the cry of a wounded animal. Someone had just died.

Others, feeling that they too were about to die, imitated his cry. And their cries seemed to come from beyond the grave. Soon everyone was crying out. Wailing, groaning, cries of distress hurled into the wind and the snow.

The contagion spread to the other carriages. Hundreds of cries rose up simultaneously. Not knowing against whom we cried. Not knowing why. The death rattle of a whole convoy who felt the end upon them. We were all going to die here. All limits had been passed. No one had any strength left. And again the night would be long.

Meir Katz groaned:

"Why don't they shoot us all right away?"

That same evening, we reached our destination.

It was late at night. The guards came to unload us. The dead were abandoned in the train. Only those who could still stand were able to get out.

Meir Katz stayed in the train. The last day had been the most murderous. A hundred of us had got into the wagon. A dozen of us got out—among them, my father and I.

We had arrived at Buchenwald.

At the gate of the camp, SS officers were waiting for us. They counted us. Then we were directed to the assembly place. Orders were given us through loudspeakers:

"Form fives!" "Form groups of a hundred!" "Five paces forward!"

I held onto my father's hand—the old, familiar fear: not to lose him.

Right next to us the high chimney of the crematory oven rose up. It no longer made any impression on us. It scarcely attracted our attention.

An established inmate of Buchenwald told us that we should have a shower and then we could go into the blocks. The idea of having a hot bath fascinated me. My father was silent. He was breathing heavily beside me.

"Father," I said. "Only another moment more. Soon we can lie down—in a bed. You can rest. . . ."

He did not answer. I was so exhausted myself that his

silence left me indifferent. My only wish was to take a bath as quickly as possible and lie down in a bed.

But it was not easy to reach the showers. Hundreds of prisoners were crowding there. The guards were unable to keep any order. They struck out right and left with no apparent result. Others, without the strength to push or even to stand up, had sat down in the snow. My father wanted to do the same. He groaned.

"I can't go on. . . . This is the end. . . . I'm going to die here. . . ."

He dragged me toward a hillock of snow from which emerged human shapes and ragged pieces of blanket.

"Leave me," he said to me. "I can't go on. . . . Have mercy on me. . . . I'll wait here until we can get into the baths. . . . You can come and find me."

I could have wept with rage. Having lived through so much, suffered so much, could I leave my father to die now? Now, when we could have a good hot bath and lie down?

"Father!" I screamed. "Father! Get up from here! Immediately! You're killing yourself. . . ."

I seized him by the arm. He continued to groan.

"Don't shout, son. . . . Take pity on your old father. . . . Leave me to rest here. . . . Just for a bit, I'm so tired . . . at the end of my strength. . . ."

He had become like a child, weak, timid, vulnerable.

"Father," I said. "You can't stay here."

I showed him the corpses all around him; they too had wanted to rest here.

"I can see them, son. I can see them all right. Let them sleep. It's so long since they closed their eyes. . . . They are exhausted . . . exhausted. . . ."

His voice was tender.

I yelled against the wind:

"They'll never wake again! Never! Don't you understand?"

For a long time this argument went on. I felt that I was

not arguing with him, but with death itself, with the death that he had already chosen.

The sirens began to wail. An alert. The lights went out throughout the camp. The guards drove us toward the blocks. In a flash, there was no one left on the assembly place. We were only too glad not to have had to stay outside longer in the icy wind. We let ourselves sink down onto the planks. The beds were in several tiers. The cauldrons of soup at the entrance attracted no one. To sleep, that was all that mattered.

It was daytime when I awoke. And then I remembered that I had a father. Since the alert, I had followed the crowd without troubling about him. I had known that he was at the end, on the brink of death, and yet I had abandoned him.

I went to look for him.

But at the same moment this thought came into my mind: "Don't let me find him! If only I could get rid of this dead weight, so that I could use all my strength to struggle for my own survival, and only worry about myself." Immediately I felt ashamed of myself, ashamed forever.

I walked for hours without finding him. Then I came to the block where they were giving out black "coffee." The men were lining up and fighting.

A plaintive, beseeching voice caught me in the spine:

"Eliezer . . . my son . . . bring me . . . a drop of coffee. . . ."

I ran to him.

"Father! I've been looking for you for so long. . . . Where were you? Did you sleep? . . . How do you feel?"

He was burning with fever. Like a wild beast, I cleared a way for myself to the coffee cauldron. And I managed to carry back a cupful. I had a sip. The rest was for him. I can't forget the light of thankfulness in his eyes while he gulped it down—an animal gratitude. With those few gulps of hot water, I probably brought him more satisfaction than I had done during my whole childhood.

He was lying on a plank, livid, his lips pale and dried

up, shaken by tremors. I could not stay by him for long. Orders had been given to clear the place for cleaning. Only the sick could stay.

We stayed outside for five hours. Soup was given out. As soon as we were allowed to go back to the blocks, I ran to my father.

"Have you had anything to eat?"

"No."

"Why not?"

"They didn't give us anything . . . they said that if we were ill we should die soon anyway and it would be a pity to waste the food. I can't go on any more. . . ."

I gave him what was left of my soup. But it was with a heavy heart. I felt that I was giving it up to him against my will. No better than Rabbi Eliahou's son had I withstood the test.

He grew weaker day by day, his gaze veiled, his face the color of dead leaves. On the third day after our arrival at Buchenwald, everyone had to go to the showers. Even the sick, who had to go through last.

On the way back from the baths, we had to wait outside for a long time. They had not yet finished cleaning the blocks.

Seeing my father in the distance, I ran to meet him. He went by me like a ghost, passed me without stopping, without looking at me. I called to him. He did not come back. I ran after him:

"Father, where are you running to?"

He looked at me for a moment, and his gaze was distant, visionary; it was the face of someone else. A moment only and on he ran again.

Struck down with dysentery, my father lay in his bunk, five other invalids with him. I sat by his side, watching him, not daring to believe that he could escape death again. Nevertheless, I did all I could to give him hope.

Suddenly, he raised himself on his bunk and put his feverish lips to my ear:

"Eliezer . . . I must tell you where to find the gold and the money I buried . . . in the cellar. . . . You know. . . ."

He began to talk faster and faster, as though he were afraid he would not have time to tell me. I tried to explain to him that this was not the end, that we would go back to the house together, but he would not listen to me. He could no longer listen to me. He was exhausted. A trickle of saliva, mingled with blood, was running from between his lips. He had closed his eyes. His breath was coming in gasps.

For a ration of bread, I managed to change beds with a prisoner in my father's bunk. In the afternoon the doctor came. I went and told him that my father was very ill.

"Bring him here!"

I explained that he could not stand up. But the doctor refused to listen to anything. Somehow, I brought my father to him. He stared at him, then questioned him in a clipped voice:

"What do you want?"

"My father's ill," I answered for him. "Dysentery. . ."

"Dysentery? That's not my business. I'm a surgeon. Go on! Make room for the others."

Protests did no good.

"I can't go on, son. . . . Take me back to my bunk. . . ."

I took him back and helped him to lie down. He was shivering.

"Try and sleep a bit, father. Try to go to sleep. . . ."

His breathing was labored, thick. He kept his eyes shut. Yet I was convinced that he could see everything, that now he could see the truth in all things.

Another doctor came to the block. But my father would not get up. He knew that it was useless.

Besides, this doctor had only come to finish off the sick. I could hear him shouting at them that they were lazy and just wanted to stay in bed. I felt like leaping at his throat, strangling him. But I no longer had the courage or the strength. I was riveted to my father's deathbed. My hands hurt, I was clenching them so hard. Oh, to strangle the doctor and the others! To burn the whole world! My father's murderers! But the cry stayed in my throat.

When I came back from the bread distribution, I found my father weeping like a child:

"Son, they keep hitting me!"

"Who?"

I thought he was delirious.

"Him, the Frenchman . . . and the Pole . . . they were hitting me."

Another wound to the heart, another hate, another reason for living lost.

"Eliezer . . . Eliezer . . . tell them not to hit me. . . . I haven't done anything. . . . Why do they keep hitting me?"

I began to abuse his neighbors. They laughed at me. I promised them bread, soup. They laughed. Then they got angry; they could not stand my father any longer, they said, because he was now unable to drag himself outside to relieve himself.

The following day he complained that they had taken his ration of bread.

"While you were asleep?"

"No. I wasn't asleep. They jumped on top of me. They snatched my bread . . . and they hit me . . . again. . . . I can't stand any more, son . . . a drop of water . . . ."

I knew that he must not drink. But he pleaded with me for so long that I gave in. Water was the worst poison he could have, but what else could I do for him? With water, without water, it would all be over soon anyway. . . .

"You, at least, have some mercy on me. . . ."

Have mercy on him! I, his only son!

A week went by like this.

"This is your father, isn't it?" asked the head of the block.

"Yes."

"He's very ill."

"The doctor won't do anything for him."

"The doctor *can't* do anything for him, now. And neither can you."

He put his great hairy hand on my shoulder and added:

"Listen to me, boy. Don't forget that you're in a concentration camp. Here, every man has to fight for himself and not think of anyone else. Even of his father. Here, there are no fathers, no brothers, no friends. Everyone lives and dies for himself alone. I'll give you a sound piece of advice—don't give your ration of bread and soup to your old father. There's nothing you can do for him. And you're killing yourself. Instead, you ought to be having his ration."

I listened to him without interrupting. He was right, I thought in the most secret region of my heart, but I dared not admit it. It's too late to save your old father, I said to myself. You ought to be having two rations of bread, two rations of soup. . . .

Only a fraction of a second, but I felt guilty. I ran to find a little soup to give my father. But he did not want it. All he wanted was water.

"Don't drink water . . . have some soup. . . ."

"I'm burning . . . why are you being so unkind to me, my son? Some water. . . ."

I brought him some water. Then I left the block for roll call. But I turned around and came back again. I lay down on the top bunk. Invalids were allowed to stay in the block. So I would be an invalid myself. I would not leave my father.

There was silence all round now, broken only by groans. In front of the block, the SS were giving orders. An officer passed by the beds. My father begged me:

"My son, some water. . . . I'm burning. . . . My stomach. . . ."

"Quiet, over there!" yelled the officer.

"Eliezer," went on my father, "some water. . . ."

The officer came up to him and shouted at him to be quiet. But my father did not hear him. He went on calling me. The officer dealt him a violent blow on the head with his truncheon.

I did not move. I was afraid. My body was afraid of also receiving a blow.

Then my father made a rattling noise and it was my name: "Eliezer."

I could see that he was still breathing—spasmodically.

I did not move.

When I got down after roll call, I could see his lips trembling as he murmured something. Bending over him, I stayed gazing at him for over an hour, engraving into myself the picture of his blood-stained face, his shattered skull.

Then I had to go to bed. I climbed into my bunk, above my father, who was still alive. It was January 28, 1945.

I awoke on January 29 at dawn. In my father's place lay another invalid. They must have taken him away before dawn and carried him to the crematory. He may still have been breathing.

There were no prayers at his grave. No candles were lit to his memory. His last word was my name. A summons, to which I did not respond.

I did not weep, and it pained me that I could not weep. But I had no more tears. And, in the depths of my being, in the recesses of my weakened conscience, could I have searched it, I might perhaps have found something like—free at last!

I had to stay at Buchenwald until April eleventh. I have nothing to say of my life during this period. It no longer mattered. After my father's death, nothing could touch me any more.

I was transferred to the children's block, where there were six hundred of us.

The front was drawing nearer.

I spent my days in a state of total idleness. And I had but one desire—to eat. I no longer thought of my father or of my mother.

From time to time I would dream of a drop of soup, of an extra ration of soup. . . .

On April fifth, the wheel of history turned.

It was late in the afternoon. We were standing in the block, waiting for an SS man to come and count us. He was late in coming. Such a delay was unknown till then in the history of Buchenwald. Something must have happened.

Two hours later the loudspeakers sent out an order from the head of the camp: all the Jews must come to the assembly place.

This was the end! Hitler was going to keep his promise.

The children in our block went toward the place. There was nothing else we could do. Gustav, the head of the block, made this clear to us with his truncheon. But on the way we met some prisoners who whispered to us:

"Go back to your block. The Germans are going to shoot you. Go back to your block, and don't move."

We went back to our block. We learned on the way that the camp resistance organization had decided not to abandon the Jews and was going to prevent their being liquidated.

As it was late and there was great upheaval—innumerable Jews had passed themselves off as non-Jews—the head of the camp decided that a general roll call would take place the following day. Everybody would have to be present.

The roll call took place. The head of the camp announced that Buchenwald was to be liquidated. Ten blocks of deportees would be evacuated each day. From this moment, there would be no further distribution of bread and soup. And the evacuation began. Every day, several thousand prisoners went through the camp gate and never came back.

On April tenth, there were still about twenty thousand of us in the camp, including several hundred children. They decided to evacuate us all at once, right on until the evening. Afterward, they were going to blow up the camp.

So we were massed in the huge assembly square, in rows of five, waiting to see the gate open. Suddenly, the sirens began to wail. An alert! We went back to the blocks. It was too late to evacuate us that evening. The evacuation was postponed again to the following day.

We were tormented with hunger. We had eaten nothing

for si:: days, except a bit of grass or some potato peelings found near the kitchens.

At ten o'clock in the morning the SS scattered through the camp, moving the last victims toward the assembly place.

Then the resistance movement decided to act. Armed men suddenly rose up everywhere. Bursts of firing. Grenades exploding. We children stayed flat on the ground in the block.

The battle did not last long. Toward noon everything was quiet again. The SS had fled and the resistance had taken charge of the running of the camp.

At about six o'clock in the evening, the first American tank stood at the gates of Buchenwald.

Our first act as free men was to throw ourselves onto the provisions. We thought only of that. Not of revenge, not of our families. Nothing but bread.

And even when we were no longer hungry, there was still no one who thought of revenge. On the following day, some of the young men went to Weimar to get some potatoes and clothes—and to sleep with girls. But of revenge, not a sign.

Three days after the liberation of Buchenwald I became very ill with food poisoning. I was transferred to the hospital and spent two weeks between life and death.

One day I was able to get up, after gathering all my strength. I wanted to see myself in the mirror hanging on the opposite wall. I had not seen myself since the ghetto.

From the depths of the mirror, a corpse gazed back at me.

The look in his eyes, as they stared into mine, has never left me.

CONNECTIONS

THE MOURNER'S KADDISH

A Kaddish is a prayer praising God that is recited several times in a traditional Jewish service. The Mourner's Kaddish makes no reference to death. Instead, it praises God and looks to the divine Kingdom to come.

Recited by the mourner in public worship.

Exalted and hallowed be God's great name
In this world of His creation.
May His will be fulfilled
And His sovereignty revealed
In the days of your lifetime
And the life of the whole house of Israel
Speedily and soon,
And say, Amen.

Congregation and mourner respond:

Be His great name blessed forever,
Yea, to all eternity.

Be the name of the most Holy One blessed,
Praised and honored, extolled and glorified,
Adored and exalted supremely,

Congregation and mourner respond:

Blessed be He,

*Beyond all blessings and hymns, praises and consolations
That may be uttered in this world,
And say, Amen.

May peace abundant descend from heaven
With life for us and for all Israel,
And say, Amen.

May He who creates the harmony of the spheres
Create peace for us and for all Israel,
And say, Amen.

*On the Sabbath before Yom Kippur say instead: Far beyond

The original text of the Mourner's Kaddish appears below. The prayer is in Aramaic, a language commonly spoken in the Middle East 2000 years ago, but is written in the Hebrew alphabet. The lines are read right to left.

Recited by the mourner in public worship.

יִתְגַּדַּל וְיִתְקַדַּשׁ שְׁמֵהּ ,רַבָּא. בְּעָלְמָא דִּי־בְרָא כִרְעוּתֵהּ.
וְיַמְלִיךְ מַלְכוּתֵהּ. בְּחַיֵּיכוֹן וּבְיוֹמֵיכוֹן. וּבְחַיֵּי דְכָל־בֵּית יִשְׂרָאֵל.
בַּעֲגָלָא וּבִזְמַן קָרִיב. וְאִמְרוּ אָמֵן:

Congregation and mourner respond:

יְהֵא שְׁמֵהּ רַבָּא מְבָרַךְ. לְעָלַם וּלְעָלְמֵי עָלְמַיָּא:

יִתְבָּרַךְ. וְיִשְׁתַּבַּח. וְיִתְפָּאַר. וְיִתְרוֹמַם. וְיִתְנַשֵּׂא. וְיִתְהַדַּר.
וְיִתְעַלֶּה. וְיִתְהַלַּל. שְׁמֵהּ דְּקֻדְשָׁא

Congregation and mourner respond:

בְּרִיךְ הוּא.

*לְעֵלָּא מִן־כָּל־בִּרְכָתָא. וְשִׁירָתָא. תֻּשְׁבְּחָתָא. וְנֶחֱמָתָא. דַּאֲמִירָן
בְּעָלְמָא. וְאִמְרוּ אָמֵן:

יְהֵא שְׁלָמָא רַבָּא מִן־שְׁמַיָּא. וְחַיִּים. עָלֵינוּ וְעַל־כָּל־יִשְׂרָאֵל.
וְאִמְרוּ אָמֵן:

עוֹשֶׂה שָׁלוֹם בִּמְרוֹמָיו. הוּא יַעֲשֶׂה שָׁלוֹם. עָלֵינוּ וְעַל־כָּל־
יִשְׂרָאֵל. וְאִמְרוּ אָמֵן:

---

*On the Sabbath before Yom Kippur say instead: לְעֵלָּא לְעֵלָּא מִכָּל

Below is a transliteration of the original text of the Mourner's Kaddish. It is a guideline for how the prayer actually sounded to Eastern European Jews in the 1940s.

Recited by the mourner in public worship.

Yisgaddal v´yiskaddash sh´meih rabbo, b´ol´mo dee-v´ro ḥir´ooseih, v´yamleeḥ mal´ḥooseih, b´ḥayyeiḥon uv´yomeiḥon, uv´ḥayyei d´ḥol beis Yisroeil, ba-agolo uviz´man koreev, v´im´ru OMEIN.

Congregation and mourner respond:

Yehei sh´meih rabbo m´voraḥ, l'olam ul´ol´mei ol'mayyo.

Yisboraḥ, v´yishtabbaḥ, v´yispoar, v´yisromam, v´yisnassei, v´yis-haddar, v´yisalleh, v´yis-ḥallal, sh´meih d´koodsho.

Congregation and mourner respond:

b´reeḥ Hu,

*l´eil´lo min kol bir´ḥoso, v´sheeroso, tooshb´ḥoso, v´neḥemoso, da-ameeron b´ol´mo, v´im´ru OMEIN.

Yehei sh´lomo rabbo min sh´mayyo, v´ḥayyeem, olei´nu v´al kol Yisroeil, v´im´ru OMEIN.

Oseh sholom bim´romov, Hu ya-aseh sholom, olei´nu v´al kol Yisroeil, v´im ru OMEIN.

■ ■ ■

*On the Sabbath before Yom Kippur say instead: l'eil'lo l'eil'lo mikkol

A Spring Morning

Ida Fink

During the night there was a pouring rain, and in the morning when the first trucks drove across the bridge, the foaming Gniezna River was the dirty-yellow color of beer. At least that's how it was described by a man who was crossing this bridge—a first-class reinforced concrete bridge—with his wife and child for the last time in his life. The former secretary of the former town council heard these words with his own ears: he was standing right near the bridge and watching the Sunday procession attentively, full of concern and curiosity. As the possessor of an Aryan great-grandmother he could stand there calmly and watch them in peace. Thanks to him and to people like him, there have survived to this day shreds of sentences, echoes of final laments, shadows of the sighs of the participants in the *marches funèbres,* so common in those times.

"Listen to this," said the former secretary of the former town council, sitting with his friends in the restaurant at the railroad station—it was all over by then. "Listen to this: Here's a man facing death, and all he can think about is beer. I was speechless. And besides, how could he say that? I made a point of looking at it, the water was like water, just a little dirtier."

"Maybe the guy was just thirsty, you know?" the owner of the bar suggested, while he filled four large mugs until the foam ran over. The clock above the bar rattled and struck twelve. It was already quiet and empty in town. The rain had stopped and the sun had broken through the white puffs of clouds. The sizzle of frying meat could be heard from the kitchen. On Sunday, dinner should be as early as possible. It was clear that the SS shared that opinion. At twelve o'clock the ground in the meadow near the forest was trampled and dug up like a fresh wound. But all around it was quiet. Not even a bird called out.

When the first trucks rode across the bridge over the surging Gniezna, it was five in the morning and it was still completely dark, yet Aron could easily make out a dozen or so canvas-covered trucks. That night he must have slept soundly, deaf to everything, since he hadn't heard the rumbling of the trucks as they descended from the hills into the little town in the valley. As a rule, the rumbling of a single truck was enough to alert him in his sleep; today, the warning signals had failed him. Later, when he was already on his way, he remembered that he had been dreaming about a persistent fly, a buzzing fly, and he realized that that buzzing was the sound of the trucks riding along the high road above his house—the last house when one left the town, the first when one entered it.

They were close now, and with horrifying detachment he realized that his threshold would be the first they crossed. "In a few minutes," he thought, and slowly walked over to the bed to wake his wife and child.

The woman was no longer asleep—he met her gaze immediately, and was surprised at how large her eyes were. But the child was lying there peacefully, deep in sleep. He sat down on the edge of the bed, which sagged under his weight. He was still robust, though no longer so healthy looking as he used to be. Now he was pale and gray, and in that pallor and grayness was the mark of hunger and poverty. And terror, too, no doubt.

He sat on the dirty bedding, which hadn't been washed for a long time, and the child lay there quietly, round and large and rosy as an apple from sleep. Outside, in the street, the motors had fallen silent; it was as quiet as if poppy seeds had been sprinkled over everything.

"Mela," he whispered, "is this a dream?"

"You're not dreaming, Aron. Don't just sit there. Put something on, we'll go down to the storeroom. There's a stack of split wood there, we can hide behind it."

"The storeroom. What a joke. If I thought we could hide in the storeroom we'd have been there long ago. In the storeroom or in here, it'll make no difference."

He wanted to stand up and walk over to the window, but he was so heavy he couldn't. The darkness was already lifting. He wondered, are they waiting until it gets light? Why is it so quiet? Why doesn't it begin?

"Aron," the woman said.

Again her large eyes surprised him, and lying there on the bed in her clothing—she hadn't undressed for the night—she seemed younger, slimmer, different. Almost the way she was when he first met her, so many years ago. He stretched out his hand and timidly, gently, stroked hers. She wasn't surprised, although as a rule he was stingy with caresses, but neither did she smile. She took his hand and squeezed it firmly. He tried to look at her, but he turned away, for something strange was happening inside him. He was breathing more and more rapidly, and he knew that in a moment these rapid breaths would turn into sobs.

"If we had known," the woman said softly, "we wouldn't have had her. But how could we have known? Smarter people didn't know. She'll forgive us, Aron, won't she?"

He didn't answer. He was afraid of this rapid breathing; he wanted only to shut his eyes, put his fingers in his ears, and wait.

"Won't she, Aron?" she repeated.

Then it occurred to him that there wasn't much time left and that he had to answer quickly, that he had to answer everything and say everything that he wanted to say.

"We couldn't know," he said. "No, we wouldn't have had her, that's clear. I remember, you came to me and said, 'I'm going to have a child, maybe I should go to a doctor.' But I wanted a child, *I* wanted one. And I said, 'Don't be afraid, we'll manage it somehow. I won't be any worse than a young father.' *I* wanted her."

"If only we had a hiding place," she whispered, "if we had a hiding place everything would be different. Maybe we should hide in the wardrobe, or under the bed. No . . . it's better to just sit here."

"A shelter is often just a shelter, and not salvation. Do you remember how they took the Goldmans? All of them, the whole family. And they had a good bunker."

"They took the Goldmans, but other people managed to hide. If only we had a cellar here . . ."

"Mela," he said suddenly, "I have always loved you very much, and if you only knew—"

But he didn't finish, because the child woke up. The little girl sat there in bed, warm and sticky from her child's sleep, and rosy all over. Serious, unsmiling, she studied her parents' faces.

"Are those trucks coming for us, Papa?" she asked, and he could no longer hold back his tears. The child knew! Five years old! The age for teddy bears and blocks. Why did we have her? She'll never go to school, she'll never love. Another minute or two . . .

"Hush, darling," the woman answered, "lie still, as still as can be, like a mouse."

"So they won't hear?"

"So they won't hear."

"If they hear us, they'll kill us," said the child, and wrapped the quilt around herself so that only the tip of her nose stuck out.

How bright her eyes are, my God! Five years old! They should be shining at the thought of games, of fun. Five! She knows, and she's waiting just like us.

"Mela," he whispered, so the child wouldn't hear, "let's hide her. She's little, she'll fit in the coalbox. She's little, but she'll understand. We'll cover her with wood chips."

"No, don't torture yourself, Aron. It wouldn't help. And what would become of her then? Who would she go to? Who would take her? It will all end the same way, if not now, then the next time. It'll be easier for her with us. Do you hear them?"

He heard them clearly and he knew: time was up. He wasn't afraid. His fear left him, his hands stopped trembling. He stood there, large and solid—breathing as if he were carrying an enormous weight.

It was turning gray outside the window. Night was slipping away, though what was this new day but night, the blackest of back nights, cruel, and filled with torment.

They were walking in the direction of the railroad station, through the town, which had been washed clean by the night's pouring rain and was as quiet and peaceful as it always was on a Sunday morning.

They walked without speaking, already stripped of everything human. Even despair was mute; it lay like a death mask, frozen and silent, on the face of the crowd.

The man and his wife and child walked along the edge of the road by the sidewalk; he was carrying the little girl in his arms. The child was quiet; she looked around solemnly, with both arms wrapped around her father's neck. The man and his wife no longer spoke. They had said their last words in the house, when the door crashed open, kicked in by the boot of an SS-man. He had said then to the child, "Don't be afraid, I'll carry you in my arms." And to his wife he said, "Don't cry. Let's be calm. Let's be strong and endure this with dignity." Then they left the house for their last journey.

For three hours they stood in the square surrounded by a heavy escort. They didn't say one word. It was almost as if they had lost the power of speech. They were mute, they were deaf and blind. Once, a terrible feeling of regret tore through him when he remembered the dream, that buzzing fly, and he understood that he had overslept his life. But this, too, passed quickly; it was no longer important, it couldn't change anything. At ten o'clock they set out. His legs were tired, his hands were numb, but he didn't put the child down, not even for a minute. He knew it was only an hour or so till they reached the fields near the station—the flat green pastures, which had recently become the mass grave of the murdered. He also recalled that years ago he used to meet Mela there, before they were husband and wife. In the evenings there was usually a strong wind, and it smelled of thyme.

The child in his arms felt heavier and heavier, but not because of her weight. He turned his head slightly and brushed the little girl's cheek with his lips. A soft, warm cheek. In an hour, or two . . .

Suddenly his heart began to pound, and his temples were drenched with sweat.

He bent towards the child again, seeking the strength that flowed from her silky, warm, young body. He still didn't know what he would do, but he did know that he had to find some chink through which he could push his child back into the world of the living. Suddenly he was thinking very fast. He was surprised to see that the trees had turned green overnight and that the river had risen; it was flowing noisily, turbulently, eddying and churning; on that quiet spring morning, it was the only sign of nature's revolt. "The water is the color of beer," he said aloud, to no one in particular. He was gathering up the colors and smells of the world that he was losing forever. Hearing his voice, the child squirmed and looked him in the eye.

"Don't be afraid," he whispered, "do what Papa tells you. Over there, near the church, there are a lot of people, they are going to pray. They are standing on the sidewalk and in the yard in front of the church. When we get there, I'm going to put you down on the ground. You're little, no one will notice you. Then you'll ask somebody to take you to Marcysia, the milkmaid, outside of town. She'll take you in. Or maybe one of those people will take you home. Do you understand what Papa said?"

The little girl looked stunned; still, he knew she had understood.

"You'll wait for us. We'll come back after the war. From the camp," he added. "That's how it has to be, darling. It has to be this way," he whispered quickly, distractedly. "That's what you'll do, you have to obey Papa."

Everything swam before his eyes; the image of the world grew blurry. He saw only the crowd in the churchyard. The sidewalk beside him was full of people, he was brushing against them with his sleeve. It was only a few steps to the churchyard gate; the crush of people was greatest there, and salvation most likely.

"Go straight to the church," he whispered and put the child down on the ground. He didn't look back, he didn't see where she ran, he walked on stiffly, at attention, his gaze fixed on the pale spring sky in which the white threads of a cloud floated like a spider web. He walked on, whispering a kind of prayer, beseeching God and men. He was still whispering when the air was rent by a furious shriek:

"Ein jüdisches Kind!"[1]

He was still whispering when the sound of a shot cracked like a stone hitting water. He felt his wife's fingers, trembling and sticky from sweat; she was seeking his hand like a blind woman. He heard her faint, whimpering moan. Then he fell silent and slowly turned around.

At the edge of the sidewalk lay a small, bloody rag. The smoke from the shot hung in the air—wispy, already blowing away. He walked over slowly, and those few steps seemed endless. He bent down, picked up the child, stroked the tangle of blond hair.

"Deine?"[2]

He answered loud and clear, "*Ja, meine.*"[3] And then softly, to her, "Forgive me."

He stood there with the child in his arms and waited for a second shot. But all he heard was a shout and he understood that they would not kill him here, that he had to keep on walking, carrying his dead child.

"Don't be afraid, I'll carry you," he whispered. The procession moved on like a gloomy, gray river flowing out to sea.

■ ■ ■

1. ***Ein jüdisches Kind!*** (German): A Jewish child!
2. ***Deine?*** (German): Yours?
3. ***Ja, meine*** (German): Yes, mine.

The Berlin-Bucharest Express

Yaffa Eliach

In Slotwina Brzesko,[1] Bronia lived near the train station and the Wehrmacht[2] headquarters. It was an advantageous location. Every night at exactly 1:20 A.M. the express train stopped for one and a half minutes, long enough for Bronia to step on or get off the train. Bronia served as a courier, delivering Aryan papers and foreign passports to Jews in various parts of Poland. She had two wonderful connections, Benjamin Sander Landau in Bochnia, who had in his possession seals from all the desirable consulates in the free world, and the ticket seller at the train station, a kind Gentile who arranged for Bronia the correct tickets needed for each occasion.

One day Bronia was traveling to Lvov[3] to bring Aryan papers and make travel arrangements for Reb Hirsch Landau and his wife, formerly from Litvatz and now living in Lvov. It is difficult to describe the despondent condition of Reb Hirsch and his wife. When Bronia entered the cold, dark little room, their faces lit up with such gratitude as she never had seen before. They were overjoyed that they were not forgotten and that their distant relative had come to their rescue. Reb Hirsch was praising the Lord that He had not forgotten His humble servant, and Mrs. Landau kept telling Bronia that if an angel had come down from heaven it would have been less of a miracle than Bronia's coming in this difficult time to rescue them. Bronia placed them on a truck and two days later they safely arrived in Tarnow.

---

1. **Slotwina Brzesko . . . Bochnia:** cities in southeastern Poland
2. **Wehrmacht:** German army
3. **Lvov:** city in Ukraine, also spelled "Lviv"

Bronia boarded the Bucharest-Berlin Express. It was December 1941. A gentle snow was falling. The train was packed with soldiers from the eastern front going home for Christmas. Next to Bronia sat a woman, a German secretary who worked at a German company in the occupied territories. Now she too was traveling home for Christmas.

At Gorodenko the train came to a sudden halt for passport control. The woman next to Bronia became very frightened. She turned to Bronia and said, "We are all dark in my family. In the past it was considered an asset. We used to be referred to as the Spanish beauties, but now my dark complexion is a curse. Each time I travel they suspect me, you know, that I am one of them. My family is one of the oldest German families. We never even intermarried with the Austrians!"

"Passports please!" Bronia was searching for her passport. "No need, comrade," the officer who checked passports said to blond, blue-eyed Bronia. "Follow me!" he ordered the German secretary. She left the compartment, never to return. Bronia finally found her passport. It was issued in Berlin, where she had lived since childhood, in her real name, Bronia Koczicki née Melchior, born in Sosnowiec. It even stated her correct date of birth. Slowly, Bronia placed the passport back into her pocketbook.

A German officer took the secretary's place and sat next to Bronia. He looked as if he were in his mid-thirties, with a very handsome face that expressed much suffering and pain. The train proceeded once more on its way. Snow was still falling and the compartment was lit by a dim light from the narrow corridor. Tears began to stream from the officer's closed eyes. He seemed to be having a nightmare. His face twitched and his lips mumbled soundless words.

He opened his eyes and turned to Bronia. The tears were still falling on his hollow cheeks. He told Bronia that he was on his way home because he could not take it any longer. "In Zhitomir it was especially horrible." He was responsible for it, too; he was in command and he gave the orders to shoot. "They assembled them all, men, women, and children. We murdered them all, all of them," he said as he wept. He showed Bronia pictures and documents to support his horrible tale. Bronia looked at them in the dim light. She felt her head spinning; she was afraid she was about to faint. How was this possible? How was it possible to murder innocent people, unsuspecting Jews dressed in their Sabbath finery? Bronia's blood was screaming, Why, why, why? She controlled her emotions, but the officer sensed her great pain, which he interpreted as sympathy for his troubled state of mind. Bronia asked for a picture for evidence. But he told her that as much as he would like to give it to her, he could not do so.

The officer asked Bronia to continue traveling with him. Her understanding and sensitivity would be of great assistance to him, he said, to ease the terrible burden he could not carry alone. Bronia replied that she would like to accompany him, but her duty did not allow her this great pleasure. At Tarnow she quickly parted from the officer and stepped down off the train into the cold, sorrowful December night.

Bronia brought back the news of Zhitomir to the town's leaders. They listened to her gruesome tale and then said, "Here it will not happen. They kill Jews only in the formerly held Russian territories because they can not distinguish between Communists and Jews. But here they know we are not Communists. We were never under Russian rule."

Bronia saw before her eyes a picture of the dead children. She questioned the spokesman of the group: "How does one mistake infants, small children, babies at their mothers' breasts for Communists?" She demanded.

"Here it will not happen," she was told over and over. "Just don't scare the people with unnecessary tales of horror."

Every night when Bronia was at home, when the Berlin-Bucharest Express rolled by, she would hear in the clickety-clack of its wheels new tales of terror, new names of other Jewish communities. Long after the train had disappeared into the frosty winter night, Bronia would clearly hear the voice of a German officer telling the gruesome tale of Zhitomir.

Based on a conversation of Rebbetzin Bronia Spira with her daughter-in-law, Dina Spira, May 10, 1976

■ ■ ■

Maus

Art Spiegelman

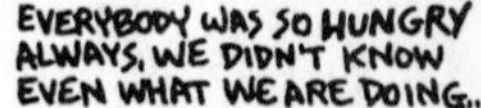
EVERYBODY WAS SO HUNGRY ALWAYS, WE DIDN'T KNOW EVEN WHAT WE ARE DOING...
IN THE MORNING FOR BREAK-FAST WE GOT ONLY A BITTER DRINK MADE FROM ROOTS.

I WOKE BEFORE EVERYBODY TO HAVE TIME TO THE TOILET AND FIND STILL SOME TEA LEFT.

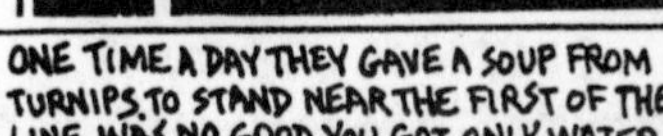
ONE TIME A DAY THEY GAVE A SOUP FROM TURNIPS. TO STAND NEAR THE FIRST OF THE LINE WAS NO GOOD. YOU GOT ONLY WATER.

MIX IT! MIX IT!
NEAR THE END WAS BETTER – SOLID THINGS TO THE BOTTOM FLOATED.

BUT TOO FAR TO THE END IT WAS ALSO NO GOOD
..BECAUSE MANY TIMES IT COULD BE NO SOUP ANYMORE.

AND ONE TIME EACH DAY THEY GAVE TO US A SMALL BREAD, CRUNCHY LIKE GLASS.

THE FLOUR THEY MIXED WITH SAWDUST TOGETHER – WE GOT ONE LITTLE BRICK OF THIS WHAT HAD TO LAST THE FULL DAY.
MOST GOBBLED IT RIGHT AWAY, BUT ALWAYS I SAVED A HALF FOR LATER.

AND IN THE EVENING WE GOT A SPOILED CHEESE OR JAM. IF WE WERE LUCKY A COUPLE TIMES A WEEK WE GOT A SAUSAGE BIG LIKE TWO OF MY FINGERS. ONLY THIS MUCH WE GOT.
IF YOU ATE HOW THEY GAVE YOU, IT WAS JUST ENOUGH TO DIE MORE SLOWLY.

EACH MORNING AND EVENING THEY MADE AN APPEL. THEY COUNTED THE LIVE ONES AND DEAD ONES TO SEE IT WASN'T ANY MISSING...
WE STOOD SOMETIMES THE WHOLE NIGHT WHILE THEY COUNTED AGAIN AND AGAIN.
ON OUR APPELS IT WAS ONE OLD GUY THERE, ALWAYS HE WAS COMPLAINING...
I DON'T BELONG HERE WITH ALL THESE YIDS AND POLACKS!
I'M A GERMAN LIKE YOU!
I HAVE MEDALS FROM THE KAISER. MY SON IS A GERMAN SOLDIER!
ONLY THEY HIT HIM AND THEY LAUGHED.
WAS HE REALLY A GERMAN?
WHO KNOWS. IT WAS GERMAN PRISONERS ALSO... BUT FOR THE GERMANS THIS GUY, WAS JEWISH!
ON ONE APPEL HE DIDN'T STAND SO STRAIGHT AND A GUARD DRAGGED HIM AWAY. I HEARD HE PUSHED HIM DOWN AND JUMPED HARD ON HIS NECK...
OR THEY SENT HIM TO THE GAS, I DON'T REMEMBER, BUT THEY FINISHED HIM AND HE NEVER ANYMORE COMPLAINED.

The Treblinka Revolt

Stanislaw Kohn

Before I arrived at Treblinka,[1] in other words before October 1, 1942, cases of rebellion on the part of Jews had been reported. Thus, for example, a Jewish youth from Warsaw who worked in one of the death companies, having seen his wife and child escorted to the gas chamber, attacked the S.S. man, Max Bill, with a knife and killed him on the spot. From that day the S.S. barracks bore the name of this Hitlerite "martyr." Neither the plate on the wall of the barracks nor the massacre of Jews after this attack deterred us. This episode encouraged us to fight and take our revenge. The Warsaw youth became our ideal.

A desire for revenge burned within us as we witnessed Hitler's extermination methods, and ripened each day and began to concretize into something precise, particularly from the moment when the fifty-year-old doctor, Choronzicki, of Warsaw, began to be active. The doctor worked in the camps as sanitation adviser, a task invented by the Germans to mock the humiliated victims even more vilely before despatching them to the gas chamber. He was a calm, cautious man who, on the surface, appeared very cold. He wandered around in his white apron with the sign of the Red Cross on his arm as in the olden days in his Warsaw consulting room, and seemed completely disinterested. But beneath his apron beat a warm Jewish heart, burning with desire for revenge.

After the infernal experiences of the day, the four instigators of the revolt met by night around his wooden bed and discussed the plans. Their first preoccupation was to get hold of dynamite and the necessary arms. These four men were the

1. **Treblinka:** A concentration camp and extermination camp located northeast of Warsaw. It is estimated that 700,000 to 900,000 prisoners were executed in Treblinka.

above-mentioned Dr. Choronzicki, the Czech army officer Zielo, naturally a Jew, Korland from Warsaw and Lubling from Silesia. After a short time, when an enlargement of the organization committee was needed, we were joined by Leon Haberman, a Warsaw artisan; Salzberg, a hatter from Kielce; Marcus, a twenty-two-year-old youth from Warsaw and the Warsaw agronomist, Sudowicz. We could procure arms either inside or outside the camp, stealing them from the German and Ukrainian S.S. We tried both methods. We began to make a study of the camp armory and the headquarters barracks. But they were guarded by Germans and there was no means of entry. At first we thought of digging a subterranean passage, but this was difficult to carry out because of the continual danger of discovery. Then we decided at all costs to make a key to the armory. This could only be done, however, if one of us could approach the iron door. It was merely a question of waiting for the propitious moment.

An opportunity soon presented itself. Something broke the lock of the armory door and the Germans were obliged to have recourse to one of the Jewish mechanics in the camp.

The Germans took the greatest precautions. The door was carried out into the laboratory, but the mechanic managed to distract the attention of the German guard for a moment and took an impression of the key in cobbler's wax. After a few days our group received a key to the armory. We hid it with the greatest care, watching for a favorable opportunity to use it.

The task of acquiring weapons outside the camp was entrusted to Dr. Choronzicki. He managed to get in contact with a Ukrainian guard who consented, naturally for a large sum of money, to buy light arms. A few of our purchases were safely smuggled in, but then something happened which put an end to our supplies and cost the life of Dr. Choronzicki. On one occasion, when carrying a large sum of money destined for the guard, he met the camp vice commandant, S.S. *Untersturmführer* Franz, a bloody murderer notorious for his sadism. By pure chance he spotted the packet of banknotes peeping out of the doctor's apron.

"Here with the money," roared the S.S. man, suspecting that the doctor was planning to leave the camp. Choronzicki lost no time and attacked him with a knife, puncturing him in the neck. Franz managed to leap out of the window and to call for help. Choronzicki, well aware of the tortures that awaited him and the dangers that threatened the whole conspiracy, swiftly swallowed a large dose of poison which the conspirators always carried on their person. The S.S. men rushed up and tried to restore him in order to take their revenge, but in vain.

In this way the instigator of the revolt died, but his death did not put an end to the matter. On the contrary, it encouraged the others to continue.

If Dr. Choronzicki had been the instigator and the head, the title of Chief of Staff must be given to Captain Zielo. The participation of this well-trained soldier greatly facilitated the realization of a task which was both difficult and complicated. In difficult moments when many of us fell a prey to resignation and abandoned all hope of a revolt, Captain Zielo continued to encourage and to incite us to carry on. When he was transferred to another part of the camp, all the plans and decisions went to him for approval, notwithstanding the danger involved in this liaison.

Engineer Galewski of Lodz was chosen to replace Dr. Choronzicki, and he, too, dedicated himself to the cause with all his heart. He was a very cautious and reserved man, typical of many of those who proved useful to our cause.

The date of the revolt was postponed several times for various reasons. The first date was fixed in April 1943, while

Dr. Choronzicki was still alive. And then the last transports of the Warsaw Jews were brought to Treblinka. From them we learned about the ghetto revolt. The Germans treated them with particular savagery; most of the trucks were full of corpses of ghetto combatants who had refused to leave the ghetto alive. Those who now arrived were no longer resigned and indifferent creatures like their predecessors.

The group decided that the hour for the revolt had arrived. In the camp were a number of so-called "court Jews," those who humiliated themselves in the service of the Germans. Some of them had a certain freedom of movement within the camp. At times they even found it possible to approach the armory. These privileged individuals were all very young. The command decided to entrust to these boys the task of expropriating a hundred hand grenades from the armory on the day of the revolt.

They proved to be well chosen for the task. Huberman, who worked in the German laundry, the shoe-black Marcus, and Jacek, a Hungarian boy of eighteen, managed to get a certain number of hand grenades. Exceptionally lithe and skillful, the fourteen-year-old boy, Salzberg, son of the above-mentioned leader, took a huge pile of S.S. uniforms as though they were being taken to the tailor, whereas the pockets of these uniforms were filled with hand grenades. The bombs had to be concealed and only appear at the last moment if the revolt was to succeed.

In the meantime our activities increased. Dr. Leichert Wengrow, chosen by the Nazis from a new batch of Jews to replace Dr. Choronzicki, eventually became a member of the committee. A Czech also joined us: Rudolf Masaryk, a relative of the late President of Czechoslovakia. He had refused to abandon his wife, a Jewess, and had accompanied her to Treblinka. Here he was among the privileged and was attached to a working party. With his own eyes he had seen his wife, who was pregnant, taken to the gas chamber. Masaryk became one of the most active members of the committee. We must also mention Rudek, the mechanic from Plok, who worked in the garage. His job was very important for our action because it was there that we hid the weapons.

Months of tension and waiting passed in this way. We looked death in the face. Thousands of men and women, completely nude, arrived daily in long files at the "Jewish State," as the Germans with their usual cynicism had christened the building which contained twelve gas chambers. *Untersturmführer* Franz continually made significant speeches in our presence: "The gas chambers will continue to function as long as a single Jew remains in the world."

The desire for revenge increased continuously. The terror-stricken eyes of the Jews being led to their death and thrust into the gas chamber called for revenge.

At last the leader, Galewski, gave the signal for the revolt. The date fixed was for Monday, August 2, 1943, at five o'clock in the afternoon. This was the plan of action: to lay an ambush for the chief murderers, to liquidate them, to disarm the warders, cut the telephone wires and then burn and destroy all the extermination plants so that they could never function again; to free the Poles from the detention camp of Treblinka a mile away, to join up with them and flee into the forest to organize a partisan band.

An atmosphere of great tension lay over the camp that Monday morning. The leaders needed all their efforts to calm people's spirits. Finally special inspectors came to see that the normal quota of work was carried out as usual in order not to arouse suspicion. Only the sixty people who had planned the coup knew the details. The activists were divided into two groups and as soon as the signal was given each group was to occupy the position assigned to it.

At one o'clock in the afternoon we got into file, as on every day, for the roll call, the last roll call in this camp because there was never to be another. But when the head of a group of workers, Galewski, told us that today work would finish an hour earlier than usual because *Scharführer* Rotner was going to Malkinia to bathe in the Bug, he winked his eye slightly as though alluding to the "bath" we had prepared for the Nazis.

At two o'clock in the afternoon the distribution of weapons began. Young Salzberg and the other boys searched their employers' huts for weapons and took them to the garage. It was very difficult to purloin the hand grenades from the armory. That day a pile of refuse was being removed from near the armory. This was very convenient but it disturbed the camp administrator, S.S. Miller, who had just arrived and wanted to sleep. The agronomist, Sudowicz, responsible for the garden, called on him with the excuse of making some decisions about plants. At the same time Marcus and Salzberg took up the carpets and beat them in front of the armory. The guards were obliged to move away for a while. At that moment the door of the armory was opened with our key and Jacek, the Hungarian boy, slipped inside, climbed onto the window sill at the end of the room, cut out a small square in the glass with a diamond and handed out the bombs and other weapons to Jacob Miller from Wlodzimierz Wolynski, who put them on his refuse cart. The arms were carried to the garage. This time the hand grenades acted as a spur.

Spirits grew agitated and no one could keep the secret. The leaders therefore decided to start the revolt an hour before the agreed time.

Punctually at four o'clock in the afternoon messages were sent to all groups with orders to assemble immediately in the garage to fetch their weapons. Rudek from Plotzk was responsible for the distribution.

Anyone coming to fetch weapons had to give the password, "Death," to which the reply was "Life." "Death-Life," "Death-Life!" Cries of enthusiasm arose as the long-hoped-for guns, revolvers and hand grenades were distributed. At the same time the chief murderers of the camp were attacked. Telephonic communication was cut and the watchtowers were set on fire with petrol. Captain Zielo attacked two S.S. guards with an ax and made his way to us to take over the command.

Near the garage stood a German armored car, but Rudek had swiftly immobilized the engine. Now the car served as a lair from which to fire on the Germans. Our gunfire felled the *Sturmführer* Kurt Majdkur and other German dogs. The armory was taken by assault and the weapons distributed. We already had two hundred armed men. The others attacked the Germans with axes and spades.

We set fire to the gas chambers, burned the faked railway station with all the notices: Bailystok-Wolkowisk, Office, Tickets, Waiting Room, etc. We burned the barracks which bore the name of Max Bill.

The flames and the reports of the firing roused the Germans who began to arrive from all sides. S.S. and police arrived from Kosow, soldiers from the nearby airfield and finally a special section of the Warsaw S.S. Orders had been given to make for the neighboring forest. Most of our fighters fell but there were many German casualties. Very few of us survived.

■ ■ ■

Mauthausen May 1945

Sonia Schreiber Weitz

It was in Mauthausen[1] that our nightmare finally came to an end. But not immediately. I remember that when we arrived at Mauthausen we had to climb a large hill to get from the train to the camp itself. Marching up that hill was really above and beyond what we were capable of. In our group of five, Edzia and I were still very sick with typhus. So the other three had to drag the two of us up that hill. I say "had to" because if you were unable to climb that hill, SS guards threw you into wagons heaped with bodies—some dead, some still alive.

Once we navigated the hill and reached the camp, there was no place to go, no place to sleep. Filled to overflowing, the camp was in total disorder. I remember black and green uniforms. There were so many levels of prisoners. And, of course, the Jews were at the lowest level.

Mostly I remember praying that they would let us go to the latrines. We had such diarrhea and vomiting! We were constantly throwing up on each other. My sister was just dragging herself around, trying to keep me alive. I think another day or two would have been too late for me.

And then it happened. Much later, I found out the date—May 4, 1945. Blanca came yelling to tell me that the *Kapos,* guards, and SS had disappeared. The next day, May 5, at 11:30 A.M., American army tanks entered Mauthausen. The prisoners themselves opened the gates to the camp and let the Americans in. And it was over!

The American soldiers were speechless with horror when they saw us. Although Allied leaders and high-ranking

---

1. **Mauthausen:** a group of camps named for the nearby Austrian village Mauthausen. The main camp and its satellites housed political dissidents, prisoners of war, and escapees from other camps as well as Jews. More than 122,000 died at these camps.

military officials had known about the death camps as early as 1942, the soldiers themselves knew very little. So these young soldiers came upon the camps totally unprepared. They entered this unimaginable world and were forever transformed by the atrocities that had been committed there.

I especially remember the expression on the face of one African-American soldier when he saw me. Sick with typhus and fever, unable to distinguish between nightmare and reality, I gazed into his horror-filled eyes.

My Black Messiah

A black GI stood by the door
(I never saw a black before)
He'll set me free before I die,
I thought, he must be the Messiah.

A black Messiah came for me . . .
He stared with eyes that didn't see,
He never heard a single word
Which hung absurd upon my tongue.

And then he simply froze in place
The shock, the horror on his face,
He didn't weep, he didn't cry
But deep within his gentle eyes
. . . A flood of devastating pain,
his innocence forever slain.

For me, with yet another dawn
I found my black Messiah gone
And on we went our separate ways
For many years without a trace.

But there's a special bond we share
Which has grown strong because we dare
To live, to hope, to smile . . . and yet
We vow *not ever to forget.*

■ ■ ■

The Yellow Star

S. B. Unsdorfer

In Night, *Eliezer's experience in the concentration camps ends at Buchenwald. One of the largest camps in Germany, Buchenwald had no gas chambers, but medical experiments were performed on the prisoners and thousands were executed or died of hunger and disease. What follows is one prisoner's detailed account of the first days after the liberation of Buchenwald in April of 1945.*

The minutes passed, and still we knelt. Then with common accord we rose from the ground. To me, it seemed that we had just arisen from *Shiva,* which is our traditional form of mourning. We ventured outside, where we found thousands of prisoners walking, dancing, marching in formation, singing, crying, and shouting in celebration.

By now the main body of tanks and armored vehicles had trundled well ahead, pushing and crushing the nation that had disgraced humanity to a just, final, and irrevocable defeat. Here and there, some prisoners, the old Buchenwaldians, were moving ahead and leaving by the main gate, armed with rifles and revolvers. Their faces were white masks, but their eyes burned with a fierce light. They were not trying to escape, nor were they intent on assisting the victorious Americans. Their one objective was to track down the murderous S.S. guards, those killers who in the hour of retribution had made a cowardly escape into the thick forest which lay close to the nearby city of Weimar. The pendulum had swung round, and now the prisoners were after the blood of their captors. Revenge, just punishment for the uniformed beasts who had slaughtered millions of innocent victims, was not to be denied.

As the avenging Buchenwaldians hurried out of the main gate, the first U.S. armored car drove into the camp proper. We rushed towards it, kissing, patting, and stroking its bulletproof body, and when the first man, an officer, thrust his steel-helmeted head out of the turret, he was pulled out by the mass of men and lifted shoulder-high. Accompanied by jubilant thousands, he was carried about the camp despite his incessant protests and demands to be returned to his troops. He was hailed by the Buchenwald prisoners as the symbol of their freedom and victory.

The great day was drawing to its close. Darkness fell. By now the camp was in possession of about one hundred S.S. guards who had been dragged in by the armed inmates. Some still wore their hated uniform; others had already donned civilian clothes which they had prepared months ahead. These erstwhile Nazi bullies were confined to a separate block near the main gates, surrounded by a posse of armed *Haeftlinge.*[1]

They cried like lost children, shouting and protesting their innocence to the angry mass of prisoners milling around the block. Some pleaded passionately that they had never been near the camp; others insisted that they were "only guards." The more inventive types claimed that their grandparents were Jews. Never has there been such a swing round from captor to captive.

When morning dawned, camp loudspeakers passed on their messages in a dozen languages, warning the liberated prisoners that the retreating S.S. had blown up the water system. It was an act of God that they did not manage to carry out their other projects, such as exploding the mines which were found all over the camp.

---

1. ***Haeftlinge*** (German): prisoners or detainees

A week elapsed before the U.S. Army managed to take charge of the camp, which included thousands of *Mussulmänner*—living corpses who were no longer able to move or even talk, so injured and seriously ill were they. Arrangements for food and water supply were made, and steps taken to dispose of the barrack full of captured S.S men.

Buchenwald was a tragic and pitiful sight in these post-war days. Day after day, new pits and huts were discovered into which thousands of dead bodies had been dumped waiting to be taken to the camp's huge crematoria. The yards inside the crematoria were packed with huge piles of dead bodies stacked twenty feet high, while scores of blocks were filled to overflowing with *Mussulmänner,* the ghastly cripples and starved-out men whose only possible salvation was a mercifully quick death and burial.

Hundreds of prisoners who in their wild hunger had rushed the kitchens and stormed the food stores, died the next day sitting on the toilets or lying on their beds. Long, long after the Nazi captors had deserted their prisoners, death raged throughout the camp and took its toll in thousands. There seemed no end to the misery and wretchedness of Buchenwald. Liberation Day had brought its own tragic end, and it broke one's heart to see that now, when aid and assistance were beginning to arrive from all parts of the globe, for many thousands of prisoners, beyond human help, they had come too late.

Meanwhile, German civilians by the hundreds were brought in daily from the nearby city of Weimar. Their task was to work in the huge kitchens, to clean and disinfect the barracks, and to dig mass graves on a steep mountain slope which stood about a mile away from the camp, and which overlooked Weimar.

I picked up a few English words and commercialized them by becoming a guide and showing visiting troops over the death camp.

"May I show you the concentration camp?" I would ask the soldiers as they streamed through the main gates. Then I would guide them around the camp, beginning with the crematoria whose stoves still held charred but recognizable bodies, on to the hospital, the *Musselmänner's* block, the punishment barracks, the dog kennels, and so on.

My reward consisted of cigarettes, chocolates, soft sweet biscuits, tinned food, and other delicious delicacies which I shared with Benzi, Grunwald, and other friends.

After "working" in the mornings, I would spend the afternoons at the cemetery watching over the Germans as they dug the graves, and myself joining other inmates who volunteered to assist in the burials.

Thousands of victims were literally chucked like old rags into the gaping mass graves. There was no time for identification attempts or even for religious rituals, in spite of the tragic scenes that frequently occurred when inmates recognized their relatives or close friends among the mass of corpses, and prayed over them.

The worthiest service I could think of performing in this huge holocaust was to say a few words of prayer. It was, indeed, all I could hope to do. Each of my visits was concluded with a quiet recital of the traditional mourners' *Kaddish.*

"May His great Name be exalted and sanctified throughout the world. . . ."

As I walked back to the camp across the broad concrete roads, built in the center of the thick forest by Jewish blood and lives, I pondered the words of the *Kaddish.*

What would happen to our Jewish nation, to our religion and heritage, after this great and tragic disaster? The face of every Jewish inmate in the camp mirrored a vivid picture of the Jewish people: a crippled and shrunken people, a race which had suffered the most tremendous spiritual, as well as physical, onslaught in the history of mankind; a race of orphans, widows, and widowers; a race of mourning fathers who had lost their sons; of saddened mothers who had their babies snatched away from their breasts; of sons who had seen their fathers, brothers, and sisters burnt to ashes while still half alive.

We had not the heroic glamor of soldiers who had died on the battlefield, or sailors drowned in the ocean; we were prisoners who had been humiliated and scorned, and now that we were free, what did the future hold?

We had lost our noblest and finest, our dearest and most precious, in the course of a callously prepared program of cold murder, destruction, and annihilation; we were a nation whose blood was shed in every country under Nazi occupation, far away from battlefields and air attacks.

Who, I wondered, would again care to hear of God, of religion, of rituals, and of observances?

I knew that the Germans would now have to supply us with food, that the British would bring drugs and medical aid, that the Americans would flood us with cigarettes, chocolates, and vitamins. But who would provide the religious serum which was so necessary to instill some spirit of Godliness into a hopelessly crushed people?

I felt the great need of my father's guidance and precept to put me on my feet again. I needed him so much, for he always knew the answers to my problems. I felt sure that he would be able to assure me that there was still a God over us, that everything that I had learned to hold and treasure was still there. But my father was dead, burned by the Nazis. Yet even now I could feel his influence.

Now that the dreadful nightmare that had started at Sered had come to an end, I had to start life afresh. How would I fare? Where should I go? Certainly I could not stay in the Devil's Chambers of Buchenwald, nor could I face the vast unknown of a foreign land.

So it came that when I was asked by the authorities after V.E. Day whether I would like to return to Czechoslovakia or emigrate to the West, I decided to return home. Maybe there was still a very faint ray of hope in me that some of my kinsmen had managed to survive. I had met people who had saved themselves at the very gates of gas chambers. Could there be? . . . Perhaps? . . . Who knew?

There were my sisters, Paula and Golda. I cherished the hope that by some miracle they might have survived the holocaust inside their bunkers in Nitra, and that I would find them safe with their families.

Bratislava was the town of my birth and my youth—the place which I loved and for which I longed whenever I left it, even for a short trip; the place where I learned to become a Jew and suffered inhuman hardships for being one. This, I felt, was the only place where I could start my life again and face the future with hope and confidence.

But strangely enough it was on the pyre of the camp, in that hellhole of Buchenwald, that I received my first injection of vitamin R—Religious Revival.

A few days before our scheduled departure for Czechoslovakia, the camp loudspeakers blazed out an announcement that the Jewish chaplain to the U.S. forces would be conducting religious services in the evening to mark the festival of *Shavuoth*—the anniversary of the receiving of the Law by the Jewish people on Mount Sinai.

Having lost my handwritten diary, as well as my *Haggadah,* during the march from Nieder-Orschel to Buchenwald, this announcement came as a pleasant yet disturbing surprise.

Since my childhood I had always looked forward eagerly to the arrival of our wonderful and inspiring festivals, and particularly so in the tragic war years. But I wondered whether we weren't being put to a test too soon. Who among those thousands of physical and mental cripples would want to attend services and prayers so soon after their tragic experiences? The Festival of the Receiving of the Torah! Within a few weeks after liberation, religion which had seemed to do so little for us, was now challenging us and our loyalties.

But just as you cannot measure the physical strength of an oppressed people, so you cannot gauge its spiritual wealth and power.

On that evening, Buchenwald staged a fantastic demonstration of faith and loyalty to God. Thousands upon thousands of liberated Jews crowded into the specially vacated block for the first postwar Jewish religious service to be held on the soil of defeated Germany. The *Mussulmänner,* the cripples, the injured, and the weak came to demonstrate to the world that the last ounce of their strength, the last drop of their blood, and the last breath of their lives belonged to God, to Torah, and to the Jewish religion.

As Chaplain Schechter intoned the Evening Prayers, all the inmates in and outside the block stood in silence, reaccepting the Torah whose people, message, and purpose

Hitler's Germany had attempted to destroy. Jewish history repeated itself. Just as our forefathers who were liberated from Egypt accepted the Law in the desert, so did we, the liberated Jews of Buchenwald, re-accept the same Law in the concentration camps of Germany.

Translated from the Yiddish by Joseph Leftwich

I Believe

I believe in the sun even when it is not shining.
I believe in love even when feeling it not.
I believe in God even when He is silent.

Inscription on the walls of a cellar in Cologne, Germany, where Jews hid from Nazis. A similar statement of faith, Ani Ma'amin (I believe) is often sung at Yom Hashoah (Holocaust Day) ceremonies.

■ ■ ■

The Trial of the Century

Tom Post

The prosecutors' task: to establish accountability for the most atrocious war crimes ever committed. How they found the evidence—and made their case.

On the morning of Nov. 21, 1945, 21 Nazi defendants filed into the dock at a somberly refurbished Palace of Justice in Nuremberg. One by one, they entered their pleas of *nicht schuldig* ("not guilty")—some quietly, others with a flash of melodrama. Reichsmarschall Herman Göring tried twice to read a prepared statement, and was cut off each time by the presiding judge. Rudolf Hess, the deputy führer who in 1941 parachuted into Scotland after a bizarre attempt to make peace with Britain, complained of abdominal cramps and had to be escorted from the courtroom.

But by afternoon a sense of solemnity had settled on the court. Robert Jackson, chief American prosecutor, rose to address the International Military Tribunal. A brilliant 53-year-old attorney who passed the bar without ever earning a law degree, Jackson had risen to become attorney general and an associate justice of the Supreme Court. That day, Jackson had a prodigious task—to establish accountability for the most atrocious war crimes ever committed. "The privilege of opening the first trial in history for crimes against the peace of the world imposes a grave responsibility," Jackson told the court. The "four great nations, flushed with victory and stung with injury, stay the hand of vengeance and voluntarily submit their captive enemies to the judgment of the law."

Troubling Questions: In trying to fix German guilt, Jackson and his counterparts from Britain, France and the Soviet Union were breaking new legal ground. Their case was ambitious and complex—made even more difficult by the need to straddle dissimilar legal systems, languages and political objectives. Put simply, the indictment charged the defendants with conspiring and launching "aggressive war," and committing war crimes and crimes against humanity. The word Nuremberg now evokes the Holocaust, but at the time the key charge was conspiracy. That focused the case beyond individuals to the criminality of the Nazi Party leadership, the High Command, the Gestapo and the SS. The trial, Jackson hoped, would satisfy the needs of justice—and offer a moral verdict on history.

But the indictment also raised troubling questions. How could the defendants be charged with crimes that weren't on any country's books at the time they were committed? Could the victors avoid substituting vengeance for justice? After all, Stalin had horrified Churchill (and amused FDR) by suggesting that leading Nazis should simply be taken out and shot. Jackson opposed summary justice; the defendants would have the right to counsel.

Proving the conspiracy charge should have been relatively simple. It required evidence that the Nazis deliberately violated treaties they had forged with other countries. With their maniacal penchant for record-keeping, the Germans had noted their preparations for war since taking over the Weimar Republic in 1933.

But where were the documents? A break in the case came in July 1945, when U.S. prosecutors learned that Alfred Rosenberg, head of the Foreign Affairs Bureau, had buried dozens of notebooks behind a wall in an old villa in Germany. Drexel Sprecher, an assistant U.S. prosecutor, got hold of the files first. "I looked at 'em and I thought, 'Jeez, where shall I start?'" he recently recalled to NEWSWEEK. He happened on a book detailing a visit to Berlin by Vidkun Quisling, a former Norwegian minister of war, not long before Germany attacked Norway. "This proved to Jackson that these files had something to do with planned aggressive war," says Sprecher. "We began to look for stuff just before the invasion of other countries." They hit pay dirt, seizing documents by the truckload. The Nazis, Jackson realized, would hang themselves.

Relying mostly on documents, rather than live witnesses, made for a powerful case. But it also ensured a protracted—and often boring—trial, dominated by hours of testimony read aloud. Horrendous crimes sometimes took on a clinical aspect. "It got so repetitious," recalls Harold Burson, then radio correspondent for the Armed Forces Network. "It was like the O. J. trial, where you got surfeited with DNA information you didn't really understand."

But there were also moments of high drama. Early in the trial, U.S. prosecutors showed film clips from Dachau, Buchenwald and Bergen-Belsen. There was excruciating testimony from camp survivors like Severina Schmaglenskaya. She described how infants, newly arrived at Auschwitz, were separated from their mothers and tossed alive into the crematory ovens; how babies born in Auschwitz were killed immediately. At one point she cried out, "In the name of all the women of Europe who became mothers in concentration camps, I would like to ask German mothers, 'Where are our children now?'"

The court also heard dispassionate accounts of terror from German witnesses. One of them was SS Gen. Otto Ohlendorf, a leader in the SD (a special intelligence service), who ended up on the stand almost serendipitously. In the course of interrogating Ohlendorf about a different defendant, U.S. prosecutor Whitney Harris discovered that the SS general had been absent from the SD during 1941. Harris asked about his activities at that time. "He said he was head of the Einsatzgruppe D," the brutal rapid-reaction force that followed the Wehrmacht into Russia. "I then asked him, 'How many men, women and children did you kill that year?'" Harris told NEWSWEEK. "He answered, 'Ninety thousand.' Their mission was to kill Jews and other 'unwanted' people. That was an event of which we had no knowledge at the time."

For sheer spectacle, few events came close to the showdown between Jackson and Göring in March 1946. After months in jail, Göring had shed a lot of weight, overcome his morphine addiction and regained his sharp faculties, bullying fellow defendants and charming the press. Jackson had already introduced enough documentary evidence to hang him; Göring had arrogantly incriminated himself during his own defense. But during the cross-examination, Jackson lost his edge. He asked redundant and open-ended questions, earning a rebuke from the court. After Jackson based a line of questioning on a mistranslated document, Göring corrected him. When he seemed to be closing in on Göring, Jackson suddenly switched subjects. Writing in The New Yorker, Janet Flanner captured the consensus when she reported that "Jackson cut a poor figure."

But he rose to eloquence in his closing argument. "If you were to say of these men that they are not guilty, it would be as true to say there has been no war, there are no slain, there has been no crime," he said. Jackson won convictions against all but three defendants. Göring cheated the hangman; hours before his scheduled execution, he took his own life. How he managed to hide the cyanide capsule for months remains a mystery. Yet his deeds, and those of his peers, have been judged—thanks to Nuremberg.

■ ■ ■

But in the night

Nelly Sachs

But in the night,
when dreams pull away
walls and ceilings with a breath of air,
the trek to the dead begins.
You search for them under the stardust—

Your longing builds up your sister—
form the elements which keep her hidden,
you bring her in
till she sighs with relief in your bed—
but your brother has gone round the corner
and your husband sits in too high a place
so that humility makes you silent—

But then—who has broken the journey—
the return begins—
like little children wailing
you are
frightened on the earth—
the death of the dead has sunk down
with the ceiling—
my head lies on your heart protectingly
love—in between you and death—

Thus dawn comes
strewn with the red seed of the sun
and night has cried itself out
into the day—

■ ■ ■

Babii Yar

Yevgeny Aleksandrovich Yevtushenko

The natural ravine of Babii Yar became a grave on September 29, 1941. In the course of thirty-six hours, the Nazis forced all the Jews in the city of Kiev to march to Babii Yar, where they were forced to strip naked and then were machine-gunned; the bodies of both the living and the dead fell into the ravine and were covered with dirt. Within two years, Babii Yar became a grave for more than 100,000 Soviet citizens, most of whom were Jewish. Just before the war ended, the Germans attempted to conceal the evidence of these massacres by removing all the bodies and burning them.

In 1961, the Soviet government announced plans to construct a sports stadium at the grave site. Finding this an insulting memorial to victims of the Holocaust, Russian poet Yevtushenko composed this poem as a protest. "Babii Yar" gained worldwide attention and precipitated the Soviet government's placement of an obelisk and a statue near the site as memorials. Unfortunately, neither monument made reference to the Jewish dead.

No monument stands over Babii Yar.
A drop sheer as a crude gravestone.
I am afraid.
                    Today I am as old in years
as all the Jewish people.
Now I seem to be
                              a Jew.

Here I plod through ancient Egypt.
Here I perish crucified, on the cross,
and to this day I bear the scars of nails.
I seem to be
Dreyfus.[1]
The Philistine[2]
is both informer and judge.
I am behind bars.
Beset on every side.
Hounded,
spat on,
slandered.
Squealing, dainty ladies in flounced Brussels lace
stick their parasols into my face.
I seem to be then
a young boy in Byelostok.
Blood runs, spilling over the floors.
The barroom rabble-rousers
give off a stench of vodka and onion.
A boot kicks me aside, helpless.
In vain I plead with these pogrom bullies.
While they jeer and shout,
"Beat the Yids. Save Russia!"
some grain marketeer beats up my mother.

---

1. **Alfred Dreyfus:** (1859–1935) A Jewish French army officer who was accused of selling military secrets to the German military. The French press and public opinion were extremely hostile to him throughout the trial, and highly antisemitic. His trial for treason started a twelve-year controversy (the Dreyfus Affair) which created a national crisis. In the end, he was finally released from prison and declared the victim of antisemitism.

2. **Philistine:** The Philistines repeatedly warred with the Israelites.

O my Russian people!
I know
you
are international to the core.
But those with unclean hands
have often made a jingle of your purest name.
I know the goodness of my land.
How vile these anti-Semites—
without a qualm
they pompously called themselves
"The Union of the Russian People"!
I seem to be
Anne Frank
transparent
as a branch in April.
And I love.
And have no need of phrases.
My need
is that we gaze into each other.
How little we can see
or smell!
We are denied the leaves,
we are denied the sky.
Yet we can do so much—
tenderly
embrace each other in a darkened room.
They're coming here?
Be not afraid. Those are the booming
sounds of spring:

spring is coming here.

Come then to me.

Quick, give me your lips.

Are they smashing down the door?

No, it's the ice breaking . . .

The wild grasses rustle over Babii Yar.

The trees look ominous,

like judges.

Here all things scream silently,

and, baring my head,

slowly I feel myself

turning gray.

And I myself

am one massive, soundless scream

above the thousand thousand buried here.

I am

each old man

here shot dead.

I am

every child

here shot dead.

Nothing in me

shall ever forget!

The "Internationale,"[3] let it

thunder

when the last anti-Semite on earth

is buried forever.

---

3. National anthem of the former U.S.S.R.

In my blood there is no Jewish blood.
In their callous rage, all anti-Semites
must hate me now as a Jew.
For that reason
I am a true Russian!

■ ■ ■

An Inner Freedom

from Man's Search for Meaning

Viktor E. Frankl

From the dark night of the concentration camp, Viktor E. Frankl awoke to a personal realization that the search for meaning is a basic human drive. Frankl witnessed fellow prisoners maintaining their humanity by believing there was still meaning to their lives and the world despite the dehumanizing humiliation of the camps. He developed his observations and personal experiences into the psychotherapeutic method of logotherapy, *or "Third School" of Viennese Psychotherapy.*

In attempting this psychological presentation and a psychopathological explanation of the typical characteristics of a concentration camp inmate, I may give the impression that the human being is completely and unavoidably influenced by his surroundings. (In this case the surroundings being the unique structure of camp life, which forced the prisoner to conform his conduct to a certain set pattern.) But what about human liberty? Is there no spiritual freedom in regard to behavior and reaction to any given surroundings? Is that theory true which would have us believe that man is no more than a product of many conditional and environmental factors—be they of a biological, psychological or sociological nature? Is man but an accidental product of these? Most important, do the prisoners' reactions to the singular world of the concentration camp prove that man cannot escape the influences of his surroundings? Does man have no choice of action in the face of such circumstances?

We can answer these questions from experience as well as on principle. The experiences of camp life show that man does have a choice of action. There were enough examples, often of a heroic nature, which proved that apathy could be overcome, irritability suppressed. Man *can* preserve a vestige of spiritual freedom, of independence of mind, even in such terrible conditions of psychic and physical stress.

We who lived in concentration camps can remember the men who walked through the huts comforting others, giving away their last piece of bread. They may have been few in number, but they offer sufficient proof that everything can be taken from a man but one thing: the last of the human freedoms—to choose one's attitude in any given set of circumstances, to choose one's own way.

And there were always choices to make. Every day, every hour, offered the opportunity to make a decision, a decision which determined whether you would or would not submit to those powers which threatened to rob you of your very self, your inner freedom; which determined whether or not you would become the plaything of circumstance, renouncing freedom and dignity to become molded into the form of the typical inmate.

Seen from this point of view, the mental reactions of the inmates of a concentration camp must seem more to us than the mere expression of certain physical and sociological conditions. Even though conditions such as lack of sleep, insufficient food and various mental stresses may suggest that the inmates were bound to react in certain ways, in the final analysis it becomes clear that the sort of person the prisoner became was the result of an inner decision, and not the result of camp influences alone. Fundamentally, therefore, any man can, even under such circumstances, decide what shall become of him—mentally and spiritually. He may retain his human dignity even in a concentration camp. Dostoevski said once, "There is only one thing that I dread: not to be worthy of my sufferings."

These words frequently came to my mind after I became acquainted with those martyrs whose behavior in camp, whose suffering and death, bore witness to the fact that the last inner freedom cannot be lost. It can be said that they were worthy of their sufferings; the way they bore their suffering was a genuine inner achievement. It is this spiritual freedom—which cannot be taken away—that makes life meaningful and purposeful.

An active life serves the purpose of giving man the opportunity to realize values in creative work, while a passive life of enjoyment affords him the opportunity to obtain fulfillment in experiencing beauty, art, or nature. But there is also purpose in that life which is almost barren of both creation and enjoyment and which admits of but one possibility of high moral behavior: namely, in man's attitude to his existence, an existence restricted by external forces. A creative life and a life of enjoyment are banned to him. But not only creativeness and enjoyment are meaningful. If there is a meaning in life at all, then there must be a meaning in suffering. Suffering is an ineradicable part of life, even as fate and death. Without suffering and death human life cannot be complete.

The way in which a man accepts his fate and all the suffering it entails, the way in which he takes up his cross, gives him ample opportunity—even under the most difficult circumstances—to add a deeper meaning to his life. It may remain brave, dignified and unselfish. Or in the bitter fight for self-preservation he may forget his human dignity and become no more than an animal. Here lies the chance for a man either to make use of or to forgo the opportunities of attaining the moral values that a difficult situation may afford him. And this decides whether he is worthy of his sufferings or not.

Do not think that these considerations are unworldly and too far removed from real life. It is true that only a few people are capable of reaching such high moral standards. Of the prisoners only a few kept their full inner liberty and obtained those values which their suffering afforded, but even one such example is sufficient proof that man's inner strength may raise him above his outward fate. Such men are not only in concentration camps. Everywhere man is confronted with fate, with the chance of achieving something through his own suffering.

Take the fate of the sick—especially those who are incurable. I once read a letter written by a young invalid, in which he told a friend that he had just found out he would not live for long, that even an operation would be of no help. He wrote further that he remembered a film he had seen in which a man was portrayed who waited for death in a courageous and dignified way. The boy had thought it a great accomplishment to meet death so well. Now—he wrote—fate was offering him a similar chance. . . .

Some details of a particular man's inner greatness may have come to one's mind, like the story of the young woman whose death I witnessed in a concentration camp. It is a simple story. There is little to tell and it may sound as if I had invented it; but to me it seems like a poem.

This young woman knew that she would die in the next few days. But when I talked to her she was cheerful in spite of this knowledge. "I am grateful that fate has hit me so hard," she told me. "In my former life I was spoiled and did not take spiritual accomplishments seriously." Pointing through the window of the hut, she said, "This tree here is the only friend I have in my loneliness." Through that window she could see just one branch of a chestnut tree, and on the branch were two blossoms. "I often talk to this tree," she said to me. I was startled and didn't quite know how to take her words. Was she delirious? Did she have occasional hallucinations?

Anxiously I asked her if the tree replied. "Yes." What did it say to her? She answered, "It said to me, 'I am here—I am here—I am life, eternal life.'"

■ ■ ■

A Cambodian Nightmare

Alex Tizon

For many Americans who did not watch the 1984 movie "The Killing Fields," what happened in Cambodia blurs with all the internecine fighting in Southeast Asia during the 1960s and '70s.

From 1975 to the end of 1978 the communist Khmer Rouge, a heavily armed peasant group of ideologues, galvanized in part by years of U.S. bombing during the Vietnam war, tried to turn Cambodia into a giant agrarian commune.

They forced city-dwellers to the countryside and systematically killed anyone who might pose a threat to their ideology: intellectuals, professionals, religious and civic leaders, indeed, anyone wearing glasses, which was considered a mark of a thinker. In the Cambodian capital of Phnom Penh, 40 percent of the population of 2 million either died or disappeared, the bodies of victims later unearthed from hundreds of mass graves outside the city.

In the countryside, people died of disease, starvation and executions.

"Under the mango trees, the skulls and bones of the old and young lay in an obscene carpet of death," writes Cambodian author Nayan Chanda.

Cambodians flooded out of the country starting in late 1978, when a Vietnamese invasion ousted the Khmer Rouge. Most fled to Thailand, whose initial response was tragic: Thai soldiers pushed back some 40,000 Cambodians through mined slopes and shot those who tried to return. Thousands died.

After an international outcry, Thailand granted haven.

Nisay Nuth, 39, was one of those forced through the mine fields. He is now an outreach counselor for the Khmer Community of Seattle-King County (Khmer is the dominant ethnic group in Cambodia). He recalls walking through forests for two days before reaching the minefields. Twenty people began the journey with him. Five survived.

"I was one of them," says Nuth, who, like other survivors, wonders with some guilt why he made it while so many others did not.

Nuth eventually made it to a Thai refugee camp, where tens of thousands of Cambodians languished for five years or longer before being resettled in a new country. . . .

The Cambodian story is not part of the active memory of the American people partly because Cambodians themselves have not fully articulated it. Most of those who would be spokesmen and spokeswomen—teachers, intellectuals, writers, artists—were killed by the Khmer Rouge.

But another reason for the silence has to do with a world view that sees nothing beneficial in dredging up painful memories, a view contrary to the Western psychiatric tenet that remembering is one of the first steps toward healing.

Patient C, a 40-year-old Cambodian man, is typical: "Why talk? You can't do anything. . . . Sometimes I have nightmares. Soldiers burying people. Dead or not dead, they would bury them. I don't like to think of that. I don't think it would help to remember. When I think of my brother, how he was killed, I get in trouble. Sometimes it makes me crazy. So I try to forget."

Cambodia's culture of fear also fostered a "societal silence." The Khmer Rouge killed dissidents without hesitation, but also killed were people who simply used the wrong word at the wrong moment. Grief was not allowed, nor anything that could be interpreted as dissatisfaction.

"The best way to survive was to shut up," says Lee Lim, a 31-year-old Cambodian who works as an Asian liaison for King County police.

Clinicians agree that the majority of Cambodian refugees suffering from depression or post-traumatic stress have not sought psychiatric help. And the relatively few who do must learn a whole new way of understanding mental health, a concept that has no equivalent in the Cambodian language.

Likewise, clinicians must work toward understanding the Cambodian world view, a largely pantheistic view that does not make easy separations between spirit, body and mind; natural and supernatural; past and present lives. Ask Cambodians if they have had conversations with dead relatives and many, perhaps the majority, will answer yes.

One remarkable characteristic documented by clinicians is the almost total absence of anger in Cambodian refugees toward their antagonists, be it Pol Pot or the Khmer Rouge or the Thai.

It was the anger of Jewish survivors of the Nazi holocaust that fueled the telling and re-telling of their story to the rest of the world.

Not so with Cambodians. And the reason is revealed in the way Cambodians understand terms such as "trauma" and "torture."

The English derivation of the word "torture," for example, is from the Latin root torquere, which means to cause to twist or turn, or to cause physical pain.

The Cambodian term, in contrast, is associated with the Buddhist concept of karma, or fate.

"The way they fit it into their consciousness is that they believe they must have done something in their past that brought this suffering on them," says Dr. David Kinzie, who runs an Indochinese mental health clinic in Portland. . . .

In the shattered families who have rallied around one another, creating new families: A young person who has lost her parents, for example, is simply taken in by another family. There are no orphans.

Cambodians bring with them a dedication to community rarely found now in Western cultures, according to Dr. Evelyn Lee, a psychiatry professor at the University of California, San Francisco who works with refugee populations. The definition of "self" in Cambodian includes community.

It can be found in their emphasis on devotion and discipline, as well as in their unshakable belief in fate, which helps in the acceptance of cataclysmic events.

Cambodians and other Southeast Asian refugees, Lee says, are products of one of the oldest cultures, cultures that emphasize trust in neighbors, gratitude for the smallest gestures, and patience with hardship—characteristics that, Lee says, Westerners would be wise to learn from.

■ ■ ■

Why *Do* They Visit?

A look at the success of the United States Holocaust Memorial Museum

John Aloysius Farrell

The GIs didn't know what the camp was for. To the young veterans of the 99th Infantry, marching through Germany in the spring of 1945, it was one more Nazi barracks on the road to Berlin: gates to be stormed and rows of one-story wooden buildings to secure. It was only inside the barbed wire that one of Sgt. Curtis Whiteway's squad members told him, "You better come with me."

"I followed him across the yard to a building—to the best of my memory, a masonry building," Whiteway recalled in an oral history published by the United States Holocaust Memorial Museum. "The windows were all sealed up. Outside . . . eight automobiles, all up on blocks. The wheels had been taken off. The exhausts were piped in through the wall of that building. We went inside the door.

"In the room . . . there was human excretion, vomit, urine, blood all over the room. I did not understand. And there were shower heads and faucets, all over the wall. One of my men called out to me. He said: 'What the hell's going on here?' He said: 'There's no water!'"

The United States Holocaust Memorial Museum opened its doors on the Mall in Washington in April 1993. Within the community of Holocaust scholars, the idea of a museum had been met with some skepticism. Many said that the building would languish, empty save for survivors and their families;

or busloads of Jewish students and temple groups. Others questioned the relevance of a memorial to European savagery amid the marble monuments of American democracy. The museum staff itself, knowing what technical marvels and poignant displays it had in store for the public, was more optimistic: The staff members thought they could draw 750,000 visitors in their first year.

It was with a strange mixture of pride and befuddled concern, then, that the Holocaust museum made a public plea last fall: It asked those planning to visit to postpone their trips to Washington. In Hollywood parlance, the museum had opened big. Inspired by word-of-mouth and generally favorable press reviews, huge mobs of people were wearing out the carpets, overloading the high-tech exhibits, and building a six-month waiting list for tour groups. In its first year on the Mall, competing with such sturdy tourist attractions as the Smithsonian Institution, the US Capitol, and the White House, a memorial to the victims of absolute Evil drew almost 2 million visitors.

Of those 2 million, according to marketing surveys, only 38 percent were Jewish. Almost two-thirds of the visitors were from places like Omaha, Nebraska, Austin, Texas, and Palos Verdes Estates, California. Native Americans came. Professional basketball players. The casts of touring Broadway shows. Why has this memorial seized the American imagination? Joan Watkins, the museum's publicist, compared it to the Vietnam Veterans Memorial. "People are willing, even on a vacation, to encounter some degree of emotional discomfort in order to learn about history," she said. That much was evident. But her answer was incomplete. As with so much else about the Holocaust, the hows and how manys are difficult enough; the whys seem insurmountable.

The museum appears, at first, to be out of place on the Mall—this Old World nightmare of shtetls and Anschluss and Zyklon-B. Outside its walls, students play volleyball, and families in shorts and tank tops emerge from the Metro to stroll the Smithsonian folklife festival, or to stake out turf with a picnic blanket. Inside the red-brick Hall of Witness—the museum's central atrium, with its steel-braced walls suggesting the crematoria and a V-shaped ramp evoking the railway sidings at Auschwitz—seemingly identical groups of Americans are herded into a metal elevator and carried off to the permanent exhibit. The elevator doors slide open to reveal a wall-size blowup of 18 American soldiers standing before a pile of calcined corpses on a pyre at the Ohrdruf concentration camp. The GIs stare, speechless and frozen in a black-and-white moment of discovery; their hands are shoved in their pockets. Fifty years later their countrymen stare back, hands in pockets, speechless as well.

It is a decision to note, this curators' choice of an opening salvo. Of all the feelings the staff could try to trigger—anger, outrage, sorrow—they chose to present instead the emotional perspective of Curtis Whiteway and his men: that of American innocence stumbling into horror. *There is no water!* Indeed, a most compelling part of this museum is its subtle juxtaposition of American ideals with the dreadful story it tells. If one looks carefully at the museum's display of a Hollerith machine—the crude data-processing device that the Nazis used to manage the shipments of humanity to the camps—you can spot the logo of the parent company of its German manufacturer: IBM. Leaving the exhibit, a visitor enters the Hall of Remembrance, a six-sided room of stone illuminated by an eternal flame and the daylight from a few unnotable windows. Those who walk its perimeter find that three of the windows have been carefully situated to frame views of the Jefferson, Lincoln, and Washington monuments.

Nothing easy awaits a visitor. The Holocaust museum sucks Americans into the drama and makes us part of the cast. It is a provocateur: insidiously offering affinities, symbols, ironies, and connections.

In an era of moral relativity, the Holocaust museum serves as a lodestone. Here there is no rationalization; here there are no excuses. Here is an absolute. And in that absolute of Evil, maybe, the prospect of an absolute Good. And maybe even God. . . .

The Holocaust museum portrays at some length the indifference, and at times anti-Semitic antagonism, that American politicians and their constituents displayed toward the plight of Europe's Jews. The US government did little to stop the slaughter—from its unrelenting embrace of prewar immigration quotas to its decision, in 1944, not to bomb the death camps and their railways.

Americans may be taught how Jesse Owens, the black sprinter, won four gold medals at the 1936 Olympics, in Berlin, thus ruining Hitler's hopes for an Aryan propaganda coup. It is left to the Holocaust museum to add to that chapter a footnote: Owens got the chance to race for his fourth gold medal because the US Olympic Committee, in fear of further offending its Nazi hosts, forced two Jewish runners—Marty Glickman and Sam Stoller—off the team for the 400-meter relay. With such parenthetical touches, the museum poses questions. What is worse? Evil? Or vacillation in its presence, in the cause of comfort, by those who know better?

Still, anyone who has walked the shore at Omaha Beach, and has seen the wide stretch of red-gold sand the GIs crossed on D-Day and the commanding position of the Nazi trenches and batteries that crowd the bluff above the landing zones, can't fail to marvel at the awesome strength of the free men and women, however slow they were to stir, who overthrew the totalitarian gangsters.

There was a time, after the war, when reverent silence was the correct response to the Holocaust. Jews had cause to dictate the terms of that response, as they had cause to demand a nation-state. But that was 50 years ago. And it may now be right for humanity to take back—respectfully—the Holocaust. To a great degree, that is what an American Holocaust museum is about. The 6 million have been mourned for half a century as Jews; the museum never forgets that the dead were Jews, but it asks us to mourn them as fellow human beings as well. . . .

With little sentimentality, the museum cites a few brave examples, plucked from the darkness of its archives, to demonstrate that man is not irredeemably evil and that acts of free will and courage are possible. Oskar Schindler is remembered, and Raoul Wallenberg, and those Danes who saved their Jewish countrymen. And most effectively, the museum allows American Holocaust survivors to tell their own stories in a series of oral histories. It's when the survivors, pausing in their tales of dread and suffering, relate—sometimes quizzically—a story of beauty or heroism, that redemption once again seems plausible.

A Jew, in prayer at one death camp, gave thanks to God that he was not like the Nazi murderers.

An American soldier describes the first words spoken by the pain-wracked survivor he would one day marry: "Noble be man, merciful and good," she said to him, quoting Goethe as she waved at the charnel house around her.

And then there is the story of Reisel's choice. As her family stood on the railroad ramp at Auschwitz, awaiting the *Selektion* of those to live or die, Reisel learned from an inmate that women with young children were sent immediately to the gas chamber. She walked over to her daughter Mina and took Mina's infant, Danny, away. To persuade Mina to give up her son, Reisel lied to her daughter—saying that women with children would have it easier in the camps and that she needed preferred treatment to survive. The last thing Reisel said, before heading to the gas chamber with her grandson, was to her other daughter, Cecilie. "Take care of your sister," she said, knowing how Mina would suffer when she learned of the consequences of the deception.

The Holocaust museum, with such stories, reaffirms an American view of the world: that the existence of a few sparkling drops of goodness, dancing in an ocean of tears, offers the possibility—though by no means the inevitability—of justice. America, founded by the skeptical theorists of the Enlightenment, is itself a test of that theory.

"The museum criticizes the American record but affirms the importance of American liberal ideals, and affirms America as a haven in and from an evil world—in keeping with traditional American ideas about the New and Old worlds," says Holocaust scholar Ken Waltzer, of Michigan State University.

In part because of such savageries as the Holocaust, the idea of God has not fared well in the 20th century. And the museum, and the topic of the Holocaust itself, may seem a strange place in which to search for divinity.

Over the last 15 years, however, colleges have found a strong demand for classes on the subject, as instructors discovered that students crave courses with a central component on morality. Raised in an increasingly secular society, many young people are drawn to questions of right and wrong.

"It is non-Jewish as well as Jewish students who pack these courses," says Waltzer. "And many colleagues who teach these courses will tell you that they stir reactions among students that these teachers get in no other courses. Students are starved . . . for moral education and discourse, for arenas where they can think and talk about fundamental human behavior. The Holocaust museum and Holocaust courses provide this," Waltzer says. "They confirm the existence of evil in the world . . . and the example of human goodness."

To a people hungry for ethical direction, the Holocaust stands as an absolute. No rationalization or deconstruction can excuse it. In an age of relativity, here is certainty. Here is Evil.

To a visitor walking the halls of the Holocaust museum, the questions—nudged along by stories like that of Reisel's sacrifice—logically follow.

If there is indeed Evil, and not merely victimization, must there not be Good, not just conditioning?

And if there is Good, may there not yet be God?

"There is not only evidence that the extreme conditions of the death camps desensitized inmates to their own suffering and that of others, there is also evidence that they became the occasion for the practice of altruistic love—from the smuggling of food to notes and words of warning, all potentially punishable by death," notes the University of Oklahoma's Ingrid Shafer. "The Christian theologian might call this the rupture of the everyday by the kingdom of God."

To some it may seem perverse to seek in such a dark episode some proof of goodness, much less God. Yet Holocaust victims undertook that search: Many went to their deaths, as an American survivor says in his oral history at the museum, with their faith intact and "their souls rinsed." Now the crowds that jam the Holocaust museum may be embarking on that search themselves.

We can never know the answer, of course. The search ultimately leads to the question, and value, of faith. But at a minimum, the Holocaust museum offers a basic moral foundation on which to build: a negative surety from which to begin. It seems a feeble contribution, yet these remain times when such guides are needed.

■ ■ ■

Nobel Peace Prize Acceptance Speech

December 10, 1986

Elie Wiesel

Wiesel was chosen for the Peace Prize by the Norwegian Nobel Committee, five people appointed by the Norwegian Parliament. The prize, considered a high honor, consisted of a gold medal, a diploma, and $270,000. At a press conference at New York City's 92nd Street Y, where he often gave lectures, Wiesel said he would use the money to set up a foundation to pay for conferences on human rights. He dedicated his award to Holocaust survivors for teaching "humankind how not to succumb to despair."

In his deeply emotional acceptance speech, Wiesel lamented that there was still much injustice in the world. "Human rights are being violated on every continent. More people are oppressed than free." But, as he pointed out, "one person of integrity can make a difference, a difference of life and death." He thanked the Nobel committee for giving him the award, adding, "No one is as capable of gratitude as one who has emerged from the kingdom of night." His fourteen-year-old son stood beside him as he spoke, a symbol that a new Jewish generation had come about in spite of the Holocaust. After the ceremony, Wiesel stood with his wife and son on the balcony of the Grand Hotel, waving to a crowd of Norwegians, who carried torches as they sang, "We Shall Overcome."

Others considered for the award included Irish rock singer Bob Geldof, who had organized concerts to aid African famine victims; Nelson and Winnie Mandela, who worked against apartheid in South Africa; and the International Olympic Committee. As an Oslo editor pointed out, although the selection of 1985 winner Yevgeny I. Chazov "probably pleased the Kremlin more than the White House, this year it will be the other way around." (Historic Documents of 1985, p. 781)

Following is the text of Elie Wiesel's speech accepting the 1986 Nobel Peace Prize:

It is with a profound sense of humility that I accept the honor you have chosen to bestow upon me. I know: your choice transcends me. This both frightens and pleases me.

It frightens me because I wonder: do I have the right to represent the multitudes who have perished? Do I have the right to accept this great honor on their behalf? I do not. That would be presumptuous. No one may speak for the dead, no one may interpret their mutilated dreams and visions.

It pleases me because I may say that this honor belongs to all the survivors and their children, and through us, to the Jewish people with whose destiny I have always identified.

I remember: it happened yesterday or eternities ago. A young Jewish boy discovered the kingdom of night. I remember his bewilderment, I remember his anguish. It all happened so fast. The ghetto. The deportation. The sealed cattle car. The fiery altar upon which the history of our people and the future of mankind were meant to be sacrificed.

I remember: he asked his father: "Can this be true? This is the 20th century, not the Middle Ages. Who would allow such crimes to be committed? How could the world remain silent?"

And now the boy is turning to me: "Tell me," he asks. "What have you done with my future? What have you done with your life?"

And I tell him that I have tried. That I have tried to keep memory alive, that I have tried to fight those who would forget. Because if we forget, we are guilty, we are accomplices.

And then I explained to him how naïve we were, that the world did know and remained silent. And that is why I swore never to be silent whenever and wherever human beings endure suffering and humiliation. We must always take sides.

Neutrality helps the oppressor, never the victim. Silence encourages the tormentor, never the tormented.

Sometimes we must interfere. When human lives are endangered, when human dignity is in jeopardy, national borders and sensitivities become irrelevant. Wherever men or women are persecuted because of their race, religion or political views, that place must—at that moment—become the center of the universe.

Of course, since I am a Jew profoundly rooted in my people's memory and tradition, my first response is to Jewish fears, Jewish needs, Jewish crises. For I belong to a traumatized generation, one that experienced the abandonment and solitude of our people. It would be unnatural for me not to make Jewish priorities my own: Israel, Soviet Jewry, Jews in Arab lands.

But there are others as important to me. Apartheid is, in my view, as abhorrent as anti-Semitism. To me, Andrei Sakharov's[1] isolation is as much of a disgrace as Iosif Begun's[2] imprisonment. As is the denial of Solidarity and its leader Lech Walesa's[3] right to dissent. And Nelson Mandela's[4] interminable imprisonment.

---

1. **Andrei Sakharov:** a Russian physicist who publicly protested the Soviet government's plan to test a hydrogen bomb. He pushed for nuclear arms reductions and spoke against the Soviet Union's repressive domestic policies and aggression toward other nations. In 1975, he was awarded the Nobel Peace Prize. From 1980 to 1986 he was exiled to the closed city of Gorky.
2. **Iosif Begun:** a Jewish dissident in the USSR who was sentenced to seven years of hard labor in 1985 and was released in 1987.
3. **Lech Walesa:** a labor activist who helped found and lead Poland's first independent trade union—"Solidarity." In 1981, the Communist government of Poland imposed martial law, outlawed Solidarity, and arrested Walesa, detaining him for nearly a year. The labor unrest grew, and Walesa negotiated with the Communist government until Solidarity was declared legal and free elections were allowed. He received the Nobel Peace Prize in 1983 and became the president of Poland in 1990.
4. **Nelson Mandela:** a black liberation group leader in South Africa who devoted his life to ending his government's apartheid policies. After years of nonviolent protest, he reacted to the 1960 Sharpeville massacre by advocating acts of sabotage against the government. In 1962, he was imprisoned and tried for treason and violent conspiracy. He was incarcerated for more than twenty-eight years and became an international symbol of opposition to apartheid. He was released in 1990, received the Nobel Peace Prize with F. W. de Klerk in 1993, and was elected president in 1994.

There is so much injustice and suffering crying out for our attention: victims of hunger, of racism and political persecution, writers and poets, prisoners in so many lands governed by the left and by the right. Human rights are being violated on every continent. More people are oppressed than free.

And then, too, there are the Palestinians to whose plight I am sensitive but whose methods I deplore. Violence and terrorism are not the answer. Something must be done about their suffering, and soon. I trust Israel, for I have faith in the Jewish people. Let Israel be given a chance, let hatred and danger be removed from her horizons, and there will be peace in and around the Holy Land.

Yes, I have faith. Faith in God and even in His creation. Without it no action would be possible. And action is the only remedy for indifference: the most insidious danger of all. Isn't this the meaning of Alfred Nobel's legacy? Wasn't his fear of war a shield against war?

There is much to be done, there is much that can be done. One person—a Raoul Wallenberg,[5] an Albert Schweitzer,[6] one person of integrity, can make a difference, a difference of life and death. As long as one dissident is in prison, our freedom will not be true. As long as one child is hungry, our lives will be filled with anguish and shame.

What all these victims need above all is to know that they are not alone; that we are not forgetting them, that when their voices are stifled we shall lend them ours, that while their freedom depends on ours, the quality of our freedom depends on theirs.

---

5. **Raoul Wallenberg:** a Swedish businessman who rescued thousands of Hungarian Jews during World War II. He was mistakenly arrested by the Soviets near the end of the war, and to this day it is uncertain whether he died in prison or is still alive.
6. **Albert Schweitzer**: a musican, theologian, philosopher, and humanitarian. He may be best known for starting a missionary hospital and leper colony in Africa, to which he devoted much of his life. In 1952, he was awarded the Nobel Peace Prize.

This is what I say to the young Jewish boy wondering what I have done with his years. It is in his name that I speak to you and that I express to you my deepest gratitude. No one is as capable of gratitude as one who has emerged from the kingdom of night.

We know that every moment is a moment of grace, every hour an offering; not to share them would mean to betray them. Our lives no longer belong to us alone; they belong to all those who need us desperately.

Thank you Chairman Aarvik. Thank you, members of the Nobel Committee. Thank you, people of Norway, for declaring on this singular occasion that our survival has meaning for mankind.

■ ■ ■

Elie Wiesel
(1928 –)

Eliezer Wiesel, one of the world's most respected authors and activists for peace, has devoted his life to documenting his experience in World War II. An author of numerous books and plays and a professor at Boston University, he has shared much of his personal life with the world through both his fiction and his nonfiction.

Born September 30, 1928, in Sighet, Romania, he was part of a community of about 15,000 Jews. He lived with his father Shlomo, a shopkeeper and respected elder of the community, his mother Sarah, and his sisters Hilda, Batya, and Tzipora in this Romanian village that was annexed to Hungary in 1940. Elie Wiesel spent his youth learning both classic and modern Hebrew, aspiring to be a rabbi. With his father's encouragement, he also studied the more secular fields of philosophy, literature, and psychology. Sighet remained surprisingly unaffected during the first years of World War II, despite daily news reports of Russian troops advancing toward Germany. The Jewish families thought they would escape the tragic fate of all the other European Jews. In April 1944, however, the Germans occupied Sighet. Wiesel's family was sent to Auschwitz, where his mother and youngest sister died. Elie and his father were sent on to Buchenwald, where his father died from starvation and abuse. Wiesel survived to be liberated by Allied troops.

After the war, Wiesel lived in Paris for over a decade, where he studied philosophy at the Sorbonne and earned a living as a choir director. His career in writing progressed when he became a correspondent for Israel's newspaper *Yedioth Ahronoth*. In 1954, he broke his self-imposed vow of silence and began writing about his experiences in the war. Wiesel has published more than thirty books since *Night.* He writes in French, and his wife translates the works into English. Many of his works incorporate direct autobiographical references, and even his fiction reveals much of his extraordinary life. He has intimately experienced what few have survived. For this reason, his stories—which stand on their own literary merit—need to be heard by the world. Wiesel, the historian, tries to link the events from the past to contemporary life, so we will not thoughtlessly repeat the same mistakes.

Seriously hurt in a 1956 car accident while visiting Manhattan, Wiesel was confined to a wheelchair for over a year. He applied for American citizenship and became a naturalized citizen in 1963. Since 1976, Wiesel has held the Andrew Mellon Chair in Humanities at Boston University. He lives in New York with his Viennese wife Marion Wiesel; they have one son.

Wiesel's honors include the Congressional Gold Medal of Achievement, the French Legion of Honor, and a number of literary prizes including the National Jewish Book Award. He chaired the United States Holocaust Memorial Council from 1978 to 1986. In 1986, Wiesel received the Nobel Peace Prize. In his acceptance speech, Wiesel emphasized one of the major themes of his work, the importance of preserving the memory of the past. "Without memory," he has written, "our existence would be barren and opaque, like a prison cell into which no light penetrates; like a tomb which rejects the living."

■ ■ ■